S0-BVF-750

LIVE POETRY

LIVE POETRY

edited by

Kathleen Sunshine Koppell

Holt, Rinehart and Winston, Inc.
New York Chicago San Francisco
Atlanta Dallas Montreal Toronto

Library of Congress Catalog Card Number: 70–141521
SBN: 03–085480–6
Printed in the United States of America
1 2 3 4 090 9 8 7 6 5 4 3 2 1

ACKNOWLEDGMENTS

For the materials copyrighted by authors, publishers, and agents, the editor is indebted to the following:

Floyce Alexander, "The Lotus Eaters." Reprinted by permission of the author and of Kayak Books, Inc.

Samuel Allen, "A Moment Please." Reprinted by permission of the author.

Jack Anderson, "The Invention of New Jersey." Reprinted by permission of the author.

Margaret Atwood, "It Is Dangerous to Read Newspapers." From *The Animals in That Country,* by Margaret Atwood. Copyright © 1968 by Oxford University Press. Reprinted by permission of Atlantic-Little, Brown and Co., and by permission of the Oxford University Press, Canadian branch. "The City Planners" and "Man with a Hook," from *The Circle Game* by Margaret Atwood, copyright by Margaret Atwood, reprinted with permission.

W. H. Auden, "The Unknown Citizen." Copyright 1940 and renewed 1968 by W. H. Auden. Reprinted from *Collected Shorter Poems 1927–1957,* by W. H. Auden, by permission of Random House, Inc., and by permission of Faber and Faber Ltd.

Art Berger, "The March on the Delta." From *American Dialog;* reprinted by permission.

Sidney Bernard, "Paraders for the Bomb." Reprinted by permission of the author.

Elizabeth Bishop, "Filling Station." Reprinted with the permission of Farrar, Straus & Giroux, Inc., from *The Complete Poems* by Elizabeth Bishop, copyright © 1955, 1969 by Elizabeth Bishop. First published in the *New Yorker.*

Robert Bly, "Watching Television" copyright ©1963 by Robert Bly; "The Great Society" copyright © 1962 by Robert Bly; "Come with Me" copyright © 1964 by Robert Bly; "Hatred of Men with Black Hair" copyright © 1966 by Robert Bly. From *The Light around the Body*, by Robert Bly. Reprinted by permission of Harper & Row, Publishers, Inc.

Richard Brautigan, "All Watched Over by Machines of Loving Grace," "The Pill versus the Springhill Mine Disaster," and " 'Star-Spangled' Nails." Reprinted from *The Pill versus the Springhill Mine Disaster* by Richard Brautigan. Copyright © 1968 by Richard Brautigan. A Seymour Lawrence Book/ Delacorte Press. Used by permission. First published by Four Seasons Foundation in its Writing series edited by Donald Allen.

Gwendolyn Brooks, "The Chicago *Defender* Sends a Man to Little Rock, Fall, 1957." From *Selected Poems* by Gwendolyn Brooks. Copyright © 1960 by Gwendolyn Brooks. Reprinted by permission of Harper & Row, Publishers, Inc.

Olga Cabral, "Another Late Edition," "Dead Sister of the Moon," "Prayer to a Computer," and "Hunger." Copyright by Olga Cabral. Reprinted by permission of the author.

Leonard Cohen, "Suzanne." © 1966 Project Seven Music, division of C.T.M.P. Inc., New York City.

e. e. cummings, "i sing of olaf," copyright 1931, 1959 by E. E. Cummings. "i thank You God for most this amazing," copyright 1950 by E. E. Cummings. "my sweet old etcetera" and "Poem, or Beauty Hurts Mr. Vinal," copyright 1926 by Horace Liveright; renewed 1954 by E. E. Cummings. "pity this busy monster,manunkind," copyright 1944 by E. E. Cummings. "the Cambridge ladies," copyright 1923, 1951 by E. E. Cummings. All reprinted from his volume *Poems 1923–1954* by permission of Harcourt Brace Jovanovich, Inc.

Peter Davison, "A Word in Your Ear on Behalf of Indifference," "The Gun Hand," and "Visions and Voices." From *Pretending to Be Asleep* by Peter Davison. Copyright © 1967, 1968, 1969, 1970 by Peter Davison. Reprinted by permission of Atheneum Publishers. "At the Site of Last Night's Fire" and "Out of Tune" from *The Breaking of the Day* by Peter Davison. Copyright © 1958, 1959, 1960, 1961, 1963, 1964 by Peter Davison. Reprinted by permission of Yale University Press.

Robert Duncan, "The Multiversity." From Robert Duncan, *Bending the Bow*. Copyright © 1968 by Robert Duncan. Reprinted by permission of New Directions Publishing Corporation.

Gail Chiarrello (Dusenbery), "The Opening Session of Congress Rock and Roll." Reprinted by permission of the author and of City Lights Books.

Bob Dylan, "A Hard Rain's A-Gonna Fall." © 1963 by M. Witmark & Sons. Used by permission of Warner Bros. Music. All Rights Reserved.

Bernard Einbond, "A Happy Yellow Window Shade." From *Mutiny*, Volume III, Number 1 (Autumn 1960), published by Mutiny Press, Box 278, Northport, N.Y. Reprinted by permission of the author.

Mari E. Evans, "The Emancipation of George-Hector (a colored turtle)" and "The Rebel." Reprinted by permission of the author.

Lawrence Ferlinghetti, "In a Surrealist Year" from *A Coney Island of the Mind*. Copyright © 1958 by Lawrence Ferlinghetti. "Assassination Raga" from *The Secret Meaning of Things*. Copyright © 1968 by Lawrence Ferlinghetti. *Tyrannus Nix?* copyright © 1969 by Lawrence Ferlinghetti. Reprinted by permission of New Directions Publishing Corporation.

Edward Field, "Unwanted," "A Bill to My Father," "The Statue of Liberty," and "Notes from a Slave Ship." Copyright © 1963 by Edward Field. Reprinted by permission of Grove Press, Inc.

Donald Finkel, "Give Way." Reprinted by permission of Charles Scribner's Sons from *The Clothing's New Emperor and Other Poems* by Donald Finkel. Copyright © 1959 by Donald Finkel. (*Poets of Today VI*).

Robert Frost, "Departmental." From *Complete Poems of Robert Frost*. Copyright 1916, 1923, 1930, 1939 by Holt, Rinehart and Winston, Inc. Copyright 1936, 1942, 1944, 1951, © 1958 by Lesley Frost Ballantine. Reprinted by permission of Holt, Rinehart and Winston, Inc.

Allen Ginsberg, "Death to Van Gogh's Ear." From *Kaddish and Other Poems* by Allen Ginsberg. Copyright © 1961 by Allen Ginsberg. Reprinted by permission of City Lights Books.

John Haines, "The Mole" copyright © 1965 by John Haines: "And When the Green Man Comes" copyright © 1961 by John Haines; "Divided, the Man Is Dreaming" copyright © 1965 by John Haines; "Horns" copyright © 1965 by John Haines; "Poem" copyright © 1965 by John Haines. Reprinted from *Winter News*, by John Haines, by permission of Wesleyan University Press. "The Great Society" copyright © 1968 by John Haines. Reprinted from *The Stone Harp*, by John Haines, by permission of Wesleyan University Press.

Anthony Hecht, "Black Boy in the Dark." Copyright © 1969, by Harper's Magazine, Inc. Reprinted from the July, 1969 issue of *Harper's Magazine* by permission of the author.

David Hilton, "In Praise of BIC Pens." From the *Chicago Review*, Vol. 20, No. 4, and Vol. 21, No. 1, p. 212. Reprinted by permission.

Frank Horne, "Kid Stuff." Reprinted by permission of the author.

Colette Inez, "Slumnight." Reprinted by permission of the author.

LeRoi Jones, "For Hettie." Copyright © 1961 by LeRoi Jones. From *Preface to a Twenty Volume Suicide Note*. Reprinted by permission of The Sterling Lord Agency.

Galway Kinnell, from "The Avenue Bearing the Initial of Christ into the New World." From *What a Kingdom It Was.* Copyright © 1960 by Galway Kinnell. Reprinted by permission of the publisher, Houghton Mifflin Company.

Stanley Kunitz, "The War against the Trees." Copyright © 1957 by Stanley Kunitz. From *Selected Poems 1928–1958* by Stanley Kunitz. Reprinted by permission of Atlantic-Little, Brown and Co.

Carl Larsen, "The Plot to Assassinate the Chase Manhattan Bank." Reprinted by permission of the author.

Denise Levertov, "Merritt Parkway" and "What Were They Like?" "What Were They Like?" from *The Sorrow Dance* by Denise Levertov; copyright © 1966 by Denise Levertov Goodman. "Merritt Parkway" from *The Jacob's Ladder* by Denise Levertov; copyright © 1958 by Denise Levertov Goodman. Reprinted by permission of New Directions Publishing Corporation.

Robert Lowell, "The Mouth of the Hudson." Reprinted with the permission of Farrar, Straus & Giroux, Inc., from *For the Union Dead* by Robert Lowell, copyright © 1964 by Robert Lowell.

Walter Lowenfels, "American Voices (II)" and "The Great Peace." Reprinted by permission of the author.

Alastair Macdonald, "T.V. News." Copyright © 1970 by The New York Times Company. Reprinted by permission.

Eugene McCarthy, "Ares" and "Three Bad Signs." Reprinted by permission of the author.

Thomas McGrath, "Something Is Dying Here." Reprinted by permission of the author.

Rod McKuen, "Heroes" and "Plan." Copyright © 1968 by Rod McKuen. "Silence Is Golden," copyright © 1967 by Editions Chanson Co. Reprinted from *Lonesome Cities,* by Rod McKuen, by permission of Random House, Inc.

Eve Merriam, "Landscaping," "Aesop in Washington" (Part V), "Hairy/Scary," "Tryst," and "Robin Hood." From *The Nixon Poems* by Eve Merriam. Copyright © 1970 by Eve Merriam. Reprinted by permission of the author and Atheneum Publishers. "Block Party," copyright Eve Merriam. Reprinted by permission of the author.

Arthur Miller, "Lines from California." Copyright © 1969 by Arthur Miller. Reprinted by permission of International Famous Agency for Arthur Miller.

Robert Pack, "Burning the Laboratory." Copyright © 1969 by Rutgers University, The State University of New Jersey. Reprinted by permission of Rutgers University Press, and of the author.

Marge Piercy, "Community," "Homo Faber: The Shell Game," "I Am a Light You Could Read By," "Learning Experience," "Simple-song," "The Morning Half-life Blues," "To Grow On," and "Why the Soup Tastes like the Daily

News." Copyright © 1967, 1968, 1969, by Marge Piercy. Reprinted from *Hard Loving*, by Marge Piercy, by permission of Wesleyan University Press.

Sylvia Plath, "The Thin People." Copyright © 1962 by Sylvia Plath. "Mushrooms" copyright © 1960 by Sylvia Plath. Both reprinted from *The Colossus and Other Poems*, by Sylvia Plath, by permission of Alfred A. Knopf, Inc., and Miss Olwyn Hughes.

Alastair Reid, "Curiosity." Reprinted by permission; © 1959 The New Yorker Magazine, Inc.

Kenneth Rexroth, "A Sword in a Cloud of Light." Kenneth Rexroth, *Collected Shorter Poems*. Copyright © 1956 by New Directions Publishing Corporation. Reprinted by permission of New Directions Publishing Corporation.

Theodore Roethke, "Dolor." Copyright 1943 by Modern Poetry Association, Inc., from *The Collected Poems of Theodore Roethke*. Reprinted by permission of Doubleday & Company, Inc.

Stephen Sandy, "The Woolworth Philodendron." From *Stresses in the Peaceable Kingdom*. Copyright © 1960, 1961, 1962, 1963, 1964, 1965, 1966, 1967 by Stephen Sandy. Reprinted by permission of the publisher, Houghton Mifflin Company.

Delmore Schwartz, "The True-Blue American." Copyright © 1955 by Delmore Schwartz, from the book *Summer Knowledge, New and Selected Poems 1938–1958* by Delmore Schwartz. Reprinted by permission of Doubleday & Company, Inc.

F.R. Scott, "Examiner." Reprinted by permission of the author.

Harvey Shapiro, "In Our Day." Copyright © 1969, by Harper's Magazine, Inc. Reprinted from the October, 1969 issue of *Harper's Magazine* by permission of the author. "National Cold Storage Company." Copyright © 1964 by Harvey Shapiro. Reprinted from *Battle Report*, by Harvey Shapiro, by permission of Wesleyan University Press, and by permission of the author.

Karl Shapiro, "The Conscientious Objector." Copyright 1947 by Karl Shapiro. Reprinted from *Selected Poems*, by Karl Shapiro, by permission of Random House, Inc.

Paul Simon, "Dangling Conversation" © 1966 by Paul Simon. "The Sound of Silence" © 1964, 1965 by Paul Simon. Used with permission of Charing Cross Music, Inc.

L. E. Sissman, "A Day in the City" copyright © 1966 by L. E. Sissman; "Sweeney to Mrs. Porter in the Spring" copyright © 1966 by L. E. Sissman. From *Dying: An Introduction*, by L. E. Sissman. "A War Requiem," from *Scattered Returns* by L. E. Sissman, copyright © 1966, 1967, 1968, 1969 by L. E. Sissman. Reprinted by permission of Atlantic-Little, Brown and Co. These poems originally appeared in *The New Yorker*.

W. D. Snodgrass, "The Men's Room in the College Chapel." Copyright © 1968 by W. D. Snodgrass. Reprinted from *After Experience*, by W. D. Snodgrass, by permission of Harper & Row, Publishers, Inc.

Gary Snyder, "A Heifer Clambers Up," "Dawn," "This Tokyo," and "Marin-An," from *The Back Country,* by Gary Snyder. Copyright © 1959, 1963, 1968 by Gary Snyder. Reprinted by permission of New Directions Publishing Corporation. "Above Pate Valley" and "Mid-August at Sourdough Mountain Lookout" are reprinted by permission of the author.

William Stafford, "Passing Remark" and from "The Move to California." From *The Rescued Year* by William Stafford. Copyright © 1960, 1961 by William Stafford, Reprinted by permission of Harper & Row, Publishers, Inc.

George Starbuck, "Of Late" from *White Paper* by George Starbuck. Copyright © 1960, 1961, 1962, 1963, 1964, 1965, 1966 by George Starbuck; originally appeared in *Poetry* (No. 1). Reprinted by permission of Atlantic-Little, Brown and Co. "Poems from a First Year in Boston: II. Outbreak of Spring" is from *Bone Thoughts* by George Starbuck. Copyright © 1960 by George Starbuck. Reprinted by permission of Yale University Press.

Dennis Trudell, "Going to Pittsburgh." Reprinted by permission of the *Wormwood Review,* Stockton, California.

David Wagoner, "The Man from the Top of the Mind." From *A Place to Stand* by David Wagoner. Reprinted by permission of Indiana University Press.

Chad Walsh, "Port Authority Terminal: 9 A.M Monday." © 1969 Chad Walsh. Reprinted from *The End of Nature,* by Chad Walsh, by permission of the author and of The Swallow Press, Inc.

Lew Welch, "Chicago Poem" and "Hiking Poem/High Sierra." Reprinted by permission of the author.

William Witherup. "Freeway." Copyright © James Boyer May 1969. First published in *Trace.* Reprinted by permission of the author.

John Woods, "Home Town." From *The Cutting Edge* by John Woods. Reprinted by permission of Indiana University Press.

James Wright, "From a Bus Window in Central Ohio, Just Before a Thunder Shower" and "Today I Was So Happy, So I Made This Poem." Copyright © 1961 by James Wright. Reprinted from *The Branch Will Not Break,* by James Wright, by permission of Wesleyan University Press. "From a Bus Window in Central Ohio, Just Before a Thunder Shower" was first published in *Poetry.*

Curtis Zahn, "Antiwarwoman." Reprinted by permission of the author.

Picture Credits

Cover: Statue of Liberty. (Adaptation.) Photography by Bruce Davidson. © 1969 Magnum Photos.

Frontispiece: United Press International Photo.

Page 5: United Press International Photo.

Page 25: United Press International Photo.

Page 47: Harbutt/Magnum from the book *America in Crisis,* published by Ridge Press and Holt, Rinehart and Winston, Inc.

Page 72: Photo: J. Everett Sherman.

Page 93: United Press International Photo.

Page 108: Photography by P. J. Griffiths. © 1969 Magnum Photos.

Page 130: United Press International Photo.

Page 150: (*top*) Photo: Peter Roll (Photo Researchers). (*bottom*) Photo: Inger Abrahamsen (Ralpho Guillumette). From *God's Own Junkyard* by Peter Blake, published by Holt, Rinehart and Winston, Inc.

Page 171: Photo: J. Everett Sherman.

Page 191: Photo: Elliott Erwitt (Magnum).

Page 196: United Press International Photo.

To Carla and Jonathan

PREFACE

Traditions are on trial. Cherished institutions are under attack. The population is divided and hostile. Communication between individuals and groups is apparently hopeless. In these troubled times, poets seem to have become, perhaps more than ever before, acute observers of contemporary life. They have escaped from their cloisters and classrooms into the harsh light of daily life through new materials, new forms, and new language. Some of their work is intended to be sung, some chanted, some screamed, some shouted, and some read in tranquil solitude. But the universal objective is somehow to communicate, to provide a link between minds in an era when isolation and antagonism have become axiomatic.

Live Poetry consists of over 125 poems and lyrics, most written during the past fifteen years. They attack the most important of contemporary concerns in contemporary language. Surrounded by dissent and demonstration, despair and disorder, these new poets are likely to deal with auto fumes, plastic greenery, peace marches, computers and politicians, garbage and tear gas. They offer vital expressions of protest against all the evils that most inflame today's youth. At the same time, they frequently return to universal concerns—love, beauty, loneliness—for vigorous reinterpretation.

Today's poets dissect all aspects of the modern dilemma, sometimes with Olympian detachment and sometimes with anger or anguish. They consider war and peace, material wealth and poverty, individuality and conformism, mechanization and nature. Their poems deal with the realities of life; stereotypes and illusions are destroyed and insights brought close to home. Thus *Live Poetry* can provoke immediate dramatic responses. To encourage spontaneous reactions to the poems (and because most touch on more than one idea), they have not been forced into a rigid classification by themes or forms.

Live Poetry offers a great variety of poetic techniques and moods. The poets, many of whom are women, represent diverse backgrounds, minority groups, and different generations. Many names will be recognized immediately: Auden, Cummings, Dylan, Frost, Ferlinghetti, Ginsberg, LeRoi Jones, Lowell, Roethke, Levertov, Paul Simon, and Eugene McCarthy. The majority, however, are young poets writing now, not yet well known but sure to be in the near future. *Live Poetry* can therefore serve as a complement to the study of poetry, either as a genre per se, or as a historical tradition. The abundance of topical ideas, attacked from refreshingly new viewpoints, makes the collection a rich source of discussion and composition materials. The collection is accompanied by a guide designed to highlight relationships between the poems themselves, as well as between the new poetry and some well-known traditional works. A number of photographs have been scattered throughout as visual reflections of the troubled times that have inspired the poets.

Live Poetry explodes into the seventies with a vitality and violence that renders it meaningful to everyone. The new poets are alive, uninhibited, and perceptive. Their fresh insights, fresh materials, and directness will surely arouse the intellect, appeal to the sense of humor, and provoke serious self-examination.

New York City
October 1970

K.S.K.

CONTENTS

LIVE POETRY

Floyce Alexander

The Lotus Eaters

(*homage to Martin Luther King, gunned down, Memphis, 4 April 1968*)

This is the dance America wanted! the dance of death.
The small animals come out of the ground,
Nothing left of them but their skins and shells,
Saying: Americans, kill what you can't
Understand. 5
Sirens! Yellow Fire-trails!
The year of the lean wolf stalks America,
Eats its own entrails, devours its children.
Immolation of the children of Asia.
Ambush of the ghost of Guevara in Bolivia. 10
And now our Gandhi, holed up in Memphis,
Taking a breath of air, leans back on the hotel
Balcony, all the sky, a southern calm, slow drawl
Of clouds, filling his eyes, before lightning cracks:

Red-necked, corpulent, born diseased, man-snake 15
Twisting its scaled body through narrow clefts
In the hills— white man! who knows how to murder,
And does, the dark-skinned man, a tattoo of bullets
Against the rough-cut cross of his body,— a lesson,
They said, chewing persimmons, spitting snuff, drinking red-eye, 20
Vagrants of spittoons, my father, uncle, grandfather, rifles
Slung over their shoulders, leaving home, glum,
ready to hunt down deer.

Samuel Allen

A Moment Please

When I gaze at the sun
I walked to the subway booth
for change for a dime.
and know that this great earth
Two adolescent girls stood there 5
alive with eagerness to know
is but a fragment from it thrown
all in their new found world
there was for them to know
in heat and flame a billion years ago, 10
they looked at me and brightly asked
"Are you Arabian?"
that then this world was lifeless
I smiled and cautiously
—for one grows cautious— 15
shook my head.
as, a billion hence,
"Egyptian?"
it shall again be
Again I smiled and shook my head 20
and walked away.
what moment is it that I am betrayed,
I've gone but seven paces now
oppressed, cast down,
and from behind comes swift the sneer 25
or warm with love or triumph?
"Or Nigger?"

A moment, please
What is it that to fury I am roused?
for still it takes a moment 30
What meaning for me
and now

in this homeless clan
  I'll turn
the dupe of space 35
  and smile
the toy of time?
  and nod my head.

Jack Anderson

The Invention of New Jersey

Place a custard stand in a garden
or in place of a custard stand
place a tumbled-down custard stand
in place of a tumbled-down custard stand
place miniature golf in a garden 5
and an advertisement for miniature golf
shaped for no apparent reason
like an old Dutch windmill
in place of a swamp
place a swamp 10

or a pizzeria called the Tower of Pizza
sporting a scale model
of the Tower of Pisa
or a water tower resembling
a roll-on deodorant 15
or a Dixie Cup factory
with a giant metal Dixie Cup on the roof

In place of wolverines, rabbits, or melons
place a vulcanizing plant
in place of a deer 20
place an iron deer
at a lawn furniture store
selling iron deer
Negro jockeys
Bavarian gnomes 25
and imitation grottoes
with electric Infants of Prague
in place of phosphorescence
of marshy ground at night
place smears of rubbish fires 30
in place of brown water with minnows
place brown water

gigantic landlords
in the doorways of apartment houses
which look like auto showrooms 35
auto showrooms which look like diners
diners which look like motels
motels which look like plastic chair covers
plastic chair covers which look like
plastic table covers which look like
                                        plastic bags 40
the mad scientist of Secaucus
invents a plastic cover
to cover the lawn
with millions of perforations
for the grass to poke through 45

In place of the straight lines of grasses
      place the straight lines of gantries
in place of lights in the window
      place lighted refineries
in place of a river 50
      place the road like a slim pair of pants
            set to dry beside a neon frankfurter
in place of New Jersey
      place a plastic New Jersey

on weekends a guy has nothing to do 55
except drive around in a convertible
counting the shoe stores
and thinking of screwing
      his date beside him
      a faintly bilious look 60
      perpetually on her face.

Margaret Atwood

It Is Dangerous to Read Newspapers

While I was building neat
castles in the sandbox,
the hasty pits were
filling with bulldozed corpses

and as I walked to the school 5
washed and combed, my feet
stepping on the cracks in the cement
detonated red bombs.

Now I am grownup
and literate, and I sit in my chair 10
as quietly as a fuse

and the jungles are flaming, the under-
brush is charged with soldiers,
the names on the difficult
maps go up in smoke 15

I am the cause, I am a stockpile of chemical
toys, my body
is a deadly gadget,
I reach out in love, my hands are guns,
my good intentions are completely lethal. 20

Even my
passive eyes transmute
everything I look at to the pocked
black and white of a war photo,
how 25
can I stop myself

It is dangerous to read newspapers.

Each time I hit a key
on my electric typewriter,
speaking of peaceful trees 30

another village explodes.

Margaret Atwood

Man with a Hook

This man I
know (about a year
ago, when he was young) blew
his arm off in the cellar
making bombs 5
to explode the robins
on the lawns.

Now he has a hook
instead of hand;

It is an ingenious 10
gadget, and comes
with various attachments:
knife for meals,
pink plastic hand for everyday
handshakes, black stuffed leather glove 15
for social functions.

I attempt pity

But, Look, he says, glittering
like a fanatic, My hook
is an improvement: 20

    and to demonstrate
lowers his arm: the steel question-
mark turns and opens,
and from his burning
cigarette 25
        unscrews
and holds the delicate
ash: a thing
precise
my clumsy tender- 30
skinned pink fingers
couldn't do.

Margaret Atwood

The City Planners

Cruising these residential Sunday
streets in dry August sunlight:
what offends us is
the sanities:
the houses in pedantic rows, the planted 5
sanitary trees, assert
levelness of surface like a rebuke
to the dent in our car door.
No shouting here, or
shatter of glass; nothing more abrupt 10
than the rational whine of a power mower
cutting a straight swath in the discouraged grass.

But though the driveways neatly
sidestep hysteria
by being even, the roofs all display 15
the same slant of avoidance to the hot sky,
certain things;
the smell of spilled oil a faint
sickness lingering in the garages,
a splash of paint on brick surprising as a bruise, 20
a plastic hose poised in a vicious
coil; even the too-fixed stare of the wide windows

give momentary access to
the landscape behind or under
the future cracks in the plaster 25

when the houses, capsized, will slide
obliquely into the clay seas, gradual as glaciers
that right now nobody notices.

That is where the City Planners
with the insane faces of political conspirators 30
are scattered over unsurveyed
territories, concealed from each other,
each in his own private blizzard;

guessing directions, they sketch
transitory lines rigid as wooden borders   35
on a wall in the white vanishing air

tracing the panic of suburb
order in a bland madness of snows.

W. H. Auden

The Unknown Citizen

(To JS/07/M/378 This Marble Monument Is Erected by the State)

He was found by the Bureau of Statistics to be
One against whom there was no official complaint,
And all the reports on his conduct agree
That, in the modern sense of an old-fashioned word, he was a saint,
For in everything he did he served the Greater Community. 5
Except for the War till the day he retired
He worked in a factory and never got fired,
But satisfied his employers, Fudge Motors Inc.
Yet he wasn't a scab or odd in his views,
For his Union reports that he paid his dues, 10
(Our report on his Union shows it was sound)
And our Social Psychology workers found
That he was popular with his mates and liked to drink.
The Press are convinced that he bought a paper every day
And that his reactions to advertisements were normal in every way. 15
Policies taken out in his name prove that he was fully insured,
And his Health-card shows he was once in hospital but left it cured.
Both Producers Research and High-Grade Living declare
He was fully sensible to the advantages of the Installment Plan
And had everything necessary to the Modern Man, 20
A phonograph, a radio, a car and a frigidaire.
Our researchers into Public Opinion are content
That he held the proper opinions for the time of year;
When there was peace, he was for peace; when there was war, he went.
He was married and added five children to the population, 25
Which our Eugenist says was the right number for a parent of his generation.
And our teachers report that he never interfered with their education.
Was he free? Was he happy? The question is absurd:
Had anything been wrong, we should certainly have heard.

Art Berger

March on the Delta

One more March
unrolls eyeballs
with scald of scenes
that are dues paid
for space to live: 5
the eagle flies high
over Mobile as the wind
prays in the street
and a tear gas fog
washes Selma faces 10
in oxides of nowhere
as we skip double dutch
in space and show
those Russians while
stars fall on Alabama 15

One more March
of whirlyhawks over Mekong
sow a notquitelethal
smog of maggots
on a defoliate scene 20
where a lone leaf sighs
a final spring
to a listless world

as our face is saved
the fig leaf is gone. 25

Sidney Bernard

Paraders for the Bomb

Full of a nitty-gritty anxiety,
I walk the plank of possible doom around me.
An unruly gust cuts the corner of
Lexington and 60th Street, loosing
a wayward placard around my feet. 5
The mustard-colored message reads,
"Bomb Hanoi." Three blond toughs, Rover Boys
for the hour, slice in and out of the
Bloomingdale's crowd. On one lapel are
"Drop It" buttons, on the other 10
"Buckley For Mayor." They made the marching
team, these three parts of the river
of patriotism that swamped Fifth Avenue,
in a tempest of cheers for war in Vietnam.
Darting into the subway, they exhale 15
a vapor of belligerent righteousness,
as they head back to the neighborhood
of their fears. The shoppers (O dreamers
of the ultimate bargain!) hardly notice
the boutonniered boys. Too busy 20
with the map of purchasing, they miss
the territory of violence around them.

Elizabeth Bishop

Filling Station

Oh, but it is dirty!
—this little filling station,
oil-soaked, oil-permeated
to a disturbing, over-all
black translucency. 5
Be careful with that match!

Father wears a dirty,
oil-soaked monkey suit
that cuts him under the arms,
and several quick and saucy 10
and greasy sons assist him
(it's a family filling station),
all quite thoroughly dirty.

Do they live in the station?
It has a cement porch 15
behind the pumps, and on it
a set of crushed and grease-
impregnated wickerwork;
on the wicker sofa
a dirty dog, quite comfy. 20

Some comic books provide
the only note of color—
of certain color. They lie
upon a big dim doily
draping a taboret 25
(part of the set), beside
a big hirsute begonia.

Why the extraneous plant?
Why the taboret?
Why, oh why, the doily? 30
(Embroidered in daisy stitch
with marguerites, I think,
and heavy with gray crochet.)

Somebody embroidered the doily.
Somebody waters the plant, 35
or oils it, maybe. Somebody
arranges the rows of cans
so that they softly say:
ESSO— SO— SO— SO
To high-strung automobiles. 40
Somebody loves us all.

Robert Bly

Come with Me

Come with me into those things that have felt this despair for
so long—
Those removed Chevrolet wheels that howl with a terrible loneliness,
Lying on their backs in the cindery dirt, like men drunk, and
naked,
Staggering off down a hill at night to drown at last in the pond.
Those shredded inner tubes abandoned on the shoulders of
thru-ways, 5
Black and collapsed bodies, that tried and burst,
And were left behind;
And the curly steel shavings, scattered about on garage benches,
Sometimes still warm, gritty when we hold them,
Who have given up, and blame everything on the government, 10
And those roads in South Dakota that feel around in the darkness . . .

Robert Bly

Hatred of Men with Black Hair

I hear voices praising Tshombe, and the Portuguese
In Angola, these are the men who skinned Little Crow!
We are all their sons, skulking
In back rooms, selling nails with trembling hands!

We distrust every person on earth with black hair; 5
We send teams to overthrow Chief Joseph's government;
We train natives to kill Presidents with blowdarts;
We have men loosening the nails on Noah's ark.

The State Department floats in the heavy jellies near the bottom
Like exhausted crustaceans, like squids who are confused, 10
Sending out beams of black light to the open sea,
Fighting their fraternal feeling for the great landlords.

We have violet rays that light up the jungles at night, showing
The friendly populations; we are teaching the children of ritual
To overcome their longing for life, and we send 15
Sparks of black light that fit the holes in the generals' eyes.

Underneath all the cement of the Pentagon
There is a drop of Indian blood preserved in snow:
Preserved from a trail of blood that once led away 20
From the stockade, over the snow, the trail now lost.

Robert Bly

The Great Society

Dentists continue to water their lawns even in the rain;
Hands developed with terrible labor by apes
Hang from the sleeves of evangelists;
There are murdered kings in the light-bulbs outside movie theaters;
The coffins of the poor are hibernating in piles of new tires. 5

The janitor sits troubled by the boiler,
And the hotel keeper shuffles the cards of insanity.
The President dreams of invading Cuba.
Bushes are growing over the outdoor grills,
Vines over the yachts and the leather seats. 10

The city broods over ash cans and darkening mortar.
On the far shore, at Coney Island, dark children
Play on the chilling beach: a sprig of black seaweed,
Shells, a skyful of birds,
While the mayor sits with his head in his hands. 15

Robert Bly

Watching Television

Sounds are heard too high for ears,
From the body cells there is an answering bay;
Soon the inner streets fill with a chorus of barks.

We see the landing craft coming in,
The black car sliding to a stop, 5
The Puritan killer loosening his guns.

Wild dogs tear off noses and eyes
And run off with them down the street—
The body tears off its own arms and throws them into the air.

The detective draws fifty-five million people into his
revolver, 10
Who sleep restlessly as in an air raid in London;
Their backs become curved in the sloping dark.

The filaments of the soul slowly separate:
The spirit breaks, a puff of dust floats up,
Like a house in Nebraska that suddenly explodes. 15

Richard Brautigan

All Watched Over by Machines of Loving Grace

I like to think (and
the sooner the better!)
of a cybernetic meadow
where mammals and computers
live together in mutually 5
programming harmony
like pure water
touching clear sky.

I like to think
(right now, please!) 10
of a cybernetic forest,
filled with pines and electronics
where deer stroll peacefully
past computers
as if they were flowers 15
with spinning blossoms.

I like to think
(it has to be!)
of a cybernetic ecology
where we are free of our labors 20
and joined back to nature,
returned to our mammal
brothers and sisters,
and all watched over
by machines of loving grace. 25

Richard Brautigan

The Pill versus the Springhill Mine Disaster

When you take your pill
it's like a mine disaster.
I think of all the people
  lost inside of you.

Richard Brautigan

"Star-Spangled" Nails

You've got
some "Star-Spangled"
  nails
in your coffin, kid.
That's what
they've done for you,
        son.

Gwendolyn Brooks

The Chicago Defender *Sends a Man to Little Rock, Fall, 1957*

In Little Rock the people bear
Babes, and comb and part their hair
And watch the want ads, put repair
To roof and latch. While wheat toast burns
A woman waters multiferns 5

Time upholds or overturns
The many, tight, and small concerns.

In Little Rock the people sing
Sunday hymns like anything,
Through Sunday pomp and polishing, 10
And after testament and tunes,
Some soften Sunday afternoons
With lemon tea and Lorna Doones.

I forecast
And I believe 15
Come Christmas Little Rock will cleave
To Christmas tree and trifle, weave,
From laugh and tinsel, texture fast.

In Little Rock is baseball; Barcarolle.
That hotness in July . . . the uniformed figures raw and
implacable 20
And not intellectual,
Batting the hotness or clawing the suffering dust.
The Open Air Concert, on the special twilight green . . .
When Beethoven is brutal or whispers to ladylike air.
Blanket-sitters are solemn, as Johann troubles to lean 25
To tell them what to mean . . .
There is love, too, in Little Rock. Soft women softly
Opening themselves in kindness,
Or, pitying one's blindness,
Awaiting one's pleasure 30

In Azure
Glory with anguished rose at the root . .
To wash away old semidiscomfitures.
They reteach purple and unsullen blue.
The wispy soils go. And uncertain 35
Half-havings have they clarified to sures.

In Little Rock they know
Not answering the telephone is a way of rejecting life,
That it is our business to be bothered, is our business
To cherish bores or boredom, be polite 40
To lies and love and many-faceted fuzziness.

I scratch my head, massage the hate-I-had.
I blink across my prim and pencilled pad.
The saga I was sent for is not down.
Because there is a puzzle in this town. 45

The biggest News I do not dare
Telegraph to the Editor's chair:
"They are like people everywhere."
The angry Editor would reply
In hundred harryings of Why. 50

And true, they are hurling spittle, rock,
Garbage and fruit in Little Rock.
And I saw coiling storm a-writhe
On bright madonnas. And a scythe
Of men harassing brownish girls. 55
(The bows and barrettes in the curls
And braids declined away from joy.)

I saw a bleeding brownish boy . . .
The lariat lynch-wish I deplored.
The loveliest lynchee was our Lord. 60

Olga Cabral

Another Late Edition

This morning the sun
for the first time in 7,000,000 years
reported late for work.
A major disaster was declared,
the major crawled underneath Manhattan 5
with his Mark Cross survival kit,
governments in Saigon
chased each other through revolving doors,
molten metal fell from the eyes of Bartholdi's Statue,
which went public and was sold at noon 10
on the Stock Exchange.
    Leaving our dinosaur footprints through the streets of cities
    what future tarpits will reveal our bones?
    what amber of what eye
    preserve this age? 15

Sheriff Rainey shifted his plug
of Red Man tobacco
and spat clear to Washington,
staining the White House and the white walls of the Capitol
with dark runnels of derision. 20
Whose blood? Whose Blood
on the Lincoln Monument?
Chaney's. Goodman's. Schwerner's.
They are dragging Walt Whitman through the streets of
        Mississippi. 25
(Bearded Jew from Brooklyn.)
They've got a rope around Abe Lincoln's neck.
(What'd we do that's wrong if we
killed two Jews and one Nigger?)

    Then all the ovens of Maidanek 30
    opened their mouths.
    I saw the enemy, a seven-year-old boy.
    I heard him screaming for his cooked eyeballs.
    I saw the granny blazing like a bundle of reeds,

heard the infant wailing in a winding-sheet of flame   35
in a village of thatched huts
hit by napalm.

The stones hate us.
The eyes are bitter.
Every tree is out to strangle us.   40
The grass mistrusts us.
We are strangers here at a million bucks a day.
They say the richest man in the world has just
foreclosed Fort Knox.
A million bucks a day can buy   45
a President. A war. A world.
But not one hair of the head of the
seven-year-old boy
in a village that went up in napalm.

Olga Cabral

Dead Sister of the Moon

Take the grand tour of the planet:
the busses are leaving for the badlands of
bottletops.
See the petrified seaports! Visit the skeletal
ships
moored on the shores of cinders.
Observe these sharp grids of footprints: 5
cybernetic man was here and gone.
He left his glyph on the dry ocean beds
in the dust of the bones of starfish.

A pity the planet's last President
could not attend his own inauguration 10
but sent a xerox copy of himself
for thalidomide posterity.
A pair of Custer's last boots took the oath of
office
and stands to this day in the Presidential
Pantheon
where a myth machine still grinds missing a
generator: 15
"It was the biggest barbecue ever!"

There was a god of this place: they called it
Huitzilopochitli or Gross National Product.
We are still decoding their history
from missing documents found in the mummy
wrappings 20
of Cabinet members. Long ago
it was all declared a disaster area
when the god fell broken and blind in the
market place
among dead croupiers and rusted bottletops.

Olga Cabral

Hunger

On the front page
of the daily fivestarfinal
*****Edition a child
is dying in the rubble
of newsprint. 5
Two eyes
assembled by dots of the wirephoto
accuse
no one. Curious.
Someone snapped a photograph: 10
This Is Famine.

What is it like
I wonder.
Five years. Or seven.
Small sack of 15
rachitic bones and
belly ballooned with vastness of
obscene death.
On famine roads
patrolled by armies of dust 20
he has lain down to
die. And claim his small room
that was too small for
life. Not a tear falls
from the glass eye 25
of the world. Someone snaps
a picture. Dying, he
accuses
no one.

"Child," 30
I say to the
wirephoto dots that are
whirling dead suns of
collapsed universes,

"Child! It was not I!" But not 35
listening. Empty holes in the
skull of space. Eyes. All the
eyes of the condemned:
black child
brown child 40
dying
on the naked roadsides of
HUNGER
in the tin cities of
HUNGER 45
on the naked sidewalks of
HUNGER
in such silence as the
TV screen goes blank and
yesterday's newsprint 50
goes stale.

Olga Cabral

Prayer to a Computer

Hear us all-wise unseeing machine-father unfeeling
hear us great holy no-sex complex monster of metal no-dream
more terrible than furnace-god of Babylonian and Carthaginian
who was simply dumb cannibal iron firebelly nothing more:

YOU 5
  of megathink artificial blockbuster brain big as a Pentagon
  clicking away the time fuse of all human fate

YOU
  of memory banks loaded with microfilm miles
  of F.B.I. filing cabinet corridors

YOU 10
  of photocell storage caves cluttered with microwaves
  of C.I.A. dream dossiers

YOU
  in whose giant beehive brain the whole human race is but 15
      one microsecond of memory

GOD OF WRATH
  of our own invention

SPY-GOD OF SPACE
  with your electronic eye beamed on every last one of us 20

GOD OF RAIN
  of fallout and scrap metal that greeneth nothing and blackeneth all

GOD THE SOWER
  who seeds cities and villages of wattle and straw with
      rain of firedeath bombs 25

GOD OF HARVESTS
  of ashes and bones

GOD OF LIGHT
of the eye-melting fireball flash of 1000 suns

GOD OF BRIMSTONE 30
of the incandescent pillar of fire

GOD OF PLAGUE
of the radioactive mushroom cloud

GOD OF HOSTS
whose messengers of vengeance are missiles without number 35

GOD OF DATA PROCESSING
who guideth the blind missile on course to its target
freezing the spine of the Angel of Death as it passeth
through space—

HEAR US ALMIGHTY PUSHBUTTON 40
HEAR US O SUPERNATURAL LIGHTNING CALCULATOR
infatuated with the order and logic of numbers and formulas
who knows all my numbers and the zip code of everyone's fate
who can come up with the answers before we have figured
the questions 45
who can solve the ultimate equation that Einstein still
ponders in his grave—

DO NOT FOLD SPINDLE OR MUTILATE
THE HUMAN HEART
DO NOT CATCH IN THE CROSSHAIRS OF HATE 50
THE LAST HUMAN CONSCIENCE
else you prove too complex for simple arithmetic
too wise to add two and two
and thine be the kingdom and the power and glory
of rust without end 55
in the asteroid junkyards of space.

Leonard Cohen

Suzanne

Suzanne takes you down
To her place near the river.
You can hear the boats go by,
You can stay the night beside her,
And you know that she's half-crazy 5
But that's why you want to be there,
And she feeds you tea and oranges
That come all the way from China,
And just when you mean to tell her
That you have no love to give her, 10
Then she gets you on her wave-length
And she lets the river answer
That you've always been her lover.

And you want to travel with her,
And you want to travel blind, 15
And you know that she can trust you
'Cause you've touched her perfect body
With your mind.

And Jesus was a sailor
When he walked upon the water 20
And he spent a long time watching
From a lonely wooden tower
And when he knew for certain
That only drowning men could see him,
He said, "All men shall be sailors, then, 25
Until the sea shall free them,"
But he, himself, was broken
Long before the sky would open.
Forsaken, almost human,
He sank beneath your wisdom 30
Like a stone.

And you want to travel with him,
And you want to travel blind,

And you think you'll maybe trust him
'Cause he touched your perfect body 35
With his mind.

Suzanne takes your hand
And she leads you to the river.
She is wearing rags and feathers
From Salvation Army counters, 40
And the sun pours down like honey
On our lady of the harbor;
And she shows you where to look
Among the garbage and the flowers.
There are heroes in the seaweed, 45
There are children in the morning,
They are leaning out for love,
And they will lean that way forever
While Suzanne, she holds the mirror.

And you want to travel with her, 50
You want to travel blind.
And you're sure that she can find you
'Cause she's touched her perfect body
With her mind.

e. e. cummings

i sing of olaf

i sing of Olaf glad and big
whose warmest heart recoiled at war:
a conscientious object-or

his well-belovéd colonel (trig
westpointer most succinctly bred) 5
took erring Olaf soon in hand;
but—though an host of overjoyed
noncoms (first knocking on the head
him) do through icy waters roll
that helplessness which others stroke 10
with brushes recently employed
anent this muddy toiletbowl,
while kindred intellects evoke
allegiance per blunt instruments—
Olaf (being to all intents 15
a corpse and wanting any rag
upon what God unto him gave)
responds, without getting annoyed
"I will not kiss your f.ing flag"

straightway the silver bird looked grave 20
(departing hurriedly to shave)

but—though all kinds of officers
(a yearning nation's blueeyed pride)
their passive prey did kick and curse
until for wear their clarion 25
voices and boots were much the worse,
and egged the firstclassprivates on
his rectum wickedly to tease
by means of skilfully applied
bayonets roasted hot with heat— 30
Olaf (upon what were once knees)
does almost ceaselessly repeat
"there is some s. I will not eat"

our president, being of which
assertions duly notified 35
threw the yellowsonofabitch
into a dungeon, where he died

Christ (of His mercy infinite)
i pray to see; and Olaf, too

preponderatingly because 40
unless statistics lie he was
more brave than me: more blond than you.

e. e. cummings

i thank You God for most this amazing

i thank You God for most this amazing
day: for the leaping greenly spirits of trees
and a blue true dream of sky; and for everything
which is natural which is infinite which is yes

(i who have died am alive again today, 5
and this is the sun's birthday; this is the birth
day of life and of love and wings: and of the gay
great happening illimitably earth)

how should tasting touching hearing seeing
breathing any–lifted from the no 10
of all nothing–human merely being
doubt unimaginable You?

(now the ears of my ears awake and
now the eyes of my eyes are opened)

e. e. cummings

my sweet old etcetera

my sweet old etcetera
aunt lucy during the recent

war could and what
is more did tell you just
what everybody was fighting 5

for,
my sister

isabel created hundreds
(and
hundreds)of socks not to 10
mention shirts fleaproof earwarmers

etcetera wristers etcetera, my
mother hoped that

i would die etcetera
bravely of course my father used 15
to become hoarse talking about how it was
a privilege and if only he
could meanwhile my

self etcetera lay quietly
in the deep mud et 20

cetera
(dreaming,
et
 cetera, of
Your smile 25
eyes knees and of your Etcetera)

e. e. cummings

pity this busy monster, manunkind

pity this busy monster,manunkind,

not. Progress is a comfortable disease:
your victim(death and life safely beyond)

plays with the bigness of his littleness
—electrons deify one razorblade 5
into a mountainrange;lenses extend

unwish through curving wherewhen till unwish
returns on its unself.
A world of made
is not a world of born—pity poor flesh 10

and trees,poor stars and stones,but never this
fine specimen of hypermagical

ultraomnipotence. We doctors know

a hopeless case if—listen:there's a hell
of a good universe next door;let's go 15

e. e. cummings

poem, or beauty hurts mr. vinal

take it from me kiddo
believe me
my country, 'tis of

you, land of the Cluett
Shirt Boston Garter and Spearmint 5
Girl With The Wrigley Eyes (of you
land of the Arrow Ide
and Earl &
Wilson
Collars) of you i 10
sing: land of Abraham Lincoln and Lydia E. Pinkham,
land above all of Just Add Hot Water And Serve—
from every B.V.D.

let freedom ring

amen. i do however protest, anent the un 15
-spontaneous and otherwise scented merde which
greets one(Everywhere Why) as divine poesy per
that and this radically defunct periodical. i would

suggest that certain ideas gestures
rhymes, like Gillette Razor Blades 20
having been used and reused
to the mystical moment of dullness emphatically are
Not To Be Resharpened. (Case in point

if we are to believe these gently O sweetly
melancholy trillers amid the thrillers 25
these crepuscular violinists among my and your
skyscrapers— Helen & Cleopatra were Just Too Lovely,
The Snail's On The Thorn enter Morn and God's
In His andsoforth

do you get me?) according 30
to such supposedly indigenous
throstles Art is O World O Life
a formula: example, Turn Your Shirttails Into
Drawers and If It Isn't An Eastman It Isn't A
Kodak therefore my friends let 35
us now sing each and all fortissimo A—
mer
i

ca, I
love, 40
You.   And there're a
hun-dred-mil-lion-oth-ers, like
all of you successfully if
delicately gelded (or spaded)
gentlemen(and ladies)—pretty 45

littleliverpill-
hearted-Nujolneeding-There's-A-Reason
americans (who tensetendoned and with
upward vacant eyes, painfully
perpetually crouched, quivering, upon the 50
sternly allotted sandpile
—how silently
emit a tiny violetflavoured nuisance: Odor?

ono.
comes out like a ribbon lies flat on the brush 55

e. e. cummings

the Cambridge ladies

the Cambridge ladies who live in furnished souls
are unbeautiful and have comfortable minds
(also, with the church's protestant blessings
daughters, unscented shapeless spirited)
they believe in Christ and Longfellow, both dead, 5
are invariably interested in so many things—
at the present writing one still finds
delighted fingers knitting for the is it Poles?
perhaps. While permanent faces coyly bandy
scandal of Mrs. N and Professor D 10
. . . . the Cambridge ladies do not care, above
Cambridge if sometimes in its box of
sky lavender and cornerless, the
moon rattles like a fragment of angry candy

Peter Davison

At the Site of Last Night's Fire

I scrape char off a board with a dull knife.
Unravelled into dust, black yields to gray,
And eager wood emerges from its mask.
Once it is stripped, the wood glows naked as bone,
Charged with light, suited to hands again. 5

To comfort this unstrung household, tiles of carbon
Clothed the sweet pine in velvet, muffled all
The liveliness that leaped within the wood
Through post and beam. Is it a fact that fire
Yesterday prowled up the stairs, munched at a floor, 10
Crumpled a roof, and tempted four upright walls
To tilt themselves into this last embrace?

Within my clothes I shiver at the scars
That overgrow delight and heal away
The marks, where bumbling flame has licked my face. 15

Peter Davison

A Word in Your Ear on Behalf of Indifference

History is sometimes salvaged by it, a civil servant
Who bows and smiles at weakness, at right and wrong;
At progress, poverty, peace and war; at victims,
Torture, and torturers. A skilled masseur,
Indifference smooths our faces into features 5
And lets our muscles work without rending each other.

Indifference-in-the-home lets tiring lovers
Share a warm bed between the defloration and
The signal for the soon-to-be-contested
Divorce to plunge both parties 10
In ice-water up to their arse.

Though we yell back and forth, "Let us erase our existence!"
"Let us scurry before the flailing winds of our senses!"
"Let us surrender into the hands of the forces!"
Indifference chimes in to discourage us from jumping. 15

My client gives us the power this side of death
To shackle ourselves, to live within our dimensions,
To ignore for hours at a time
The outrage and the dread
Of being no more than we are. 20

Peter Davison

Out of Tune

Irving, pleasant-spoken, liked by dogs,
Children, earns his neighbors' shining smiles,
The respect of spokesmen. Yet he stumbles,
Sees only glare in sun, drabness in the green
Of leaves, futility in the flight of a bird. 5
Winter sours his mouth with taste of iron.
Scent of love gives off smell of decay.
At the core of himself nothing can be heard
But thumping of blood. Thoughts are cold as slate.

Wrapped like a fly in the spiderweb of the world, 10
What would he give now to have flown
Sure as the man on skis whose swiftness leans
Against the snowy shoulder of the hill?

Peter Davison

The Gun Hand

You have been looking out for me. I held
A pistol to the ear of the Saigon captive.
It's been a busy year. I plugged the preacher
As he leaned on the lattice railing of his motel
And drilled the senator as he strode among the busboys. 5
I have aimed a thousand killers of all calibres
At television pictures, egg-hatted cops,
At the pulsing cartilage of a child's temple,
At the upstart cars that pass mine on the right.
I have squeezed so often you might think me weary, 10
But my hand is poised and clenched to squeeze again
At the next sweet target of opportunity.

Peter Davison

Visions and Voices

For days the television seared our eyes
with images of the many-widowed family.
We crouched to stare at their loosened faces, their fingers
on rosaries, the hunched and harnessed shoulders.
(We starve for what survival has to teach us.) 5
Term after term their champions had been chosen
served, shot down, reciting Aeschylus
and Tennyson. (" 'Tis not too late to seek
a newer world," and other familiar quotations.)

Too late, as usual, the latest killing 10
instructs us in our love for those who seek
more than we think of seeking. Soft in our seats
we watch the people of the long procession
reeling out across the summer landscape
to hide a body shredded and cold with bullets. 15
No one can hold his tongue: shrilled editorials,
New Year's resolutions, blurted promises
drown out the inner yelp of unmastered hounds
who press and snuffle hungrily along
the course this body leads us. At least, at night, 20
his remnants vanish in the grainy ground.

Before and after death we coursed that body.
No matter if words attacked, we could shrug them off,
but his image aroused our desire and nudged our hatred.
Slogging up mountains, seized by rapids, breasting 25
breakers, standing stripped naked by crowds,
his body sexed us. It revealed a self
our mirrors had never included. Gawky, controlled,
athletic in action, hectoring in speech,
it performed deeds that could have broken us 30
and left us with the trophies of last year's hunting-
whistles, grunts and imitated animals.

"Change," his body said— but when we heard
our voices speaking, they were not our voices.
His body has emptied the screens of our sight 35
The people are not listening to voices.

Robert Duncan

The Multiversity

not men   but heads of the hydra
his false faces in which
authority lies
hired minds of private interests
over us   5
here: Kerr (behind him, heads of the Bank of America
the Tribune,
heads of usury, heads of war)
the worm's   mouthpiece   spreads
what it wishes   its own   10
false news: 1) that the students broke into Sproul's office,
vandalizing, creating disorder; 2) that the Free Speech
Movement has no wide support, only an irresponsible min-
ority   going on strike
Chancellor Strong,   the dragon claw   15
biting his bowels, his bile
raging against the lawful demand
for right reason.
In this scene   absolute authority
the great dragon himself so confronted   20
whose scales are men officized —ossified— conscience
no longer alive in them,
the inner law silenced,   now
they call out their cops, police law,
the club, the gun, the strong arm,   25
gang-law of the state,
hired sadists of installd mediocrities.
The aging Professor, translator of fashionable surrealist
revolutionaries, muttering —
They shld not be permitted to be students; they shld   30
be in the army.
Where there is no commune,
the individual volition has no ground.
Where there is no individual freedom,   the commune
is falsified.   35

in Blake's day "old Nobodaddy"
in whose image, reduced in spirit
Kerr
(Stevenson, lying in the U.N. to save face)
He swore a great & solemn Oath 40
To kill the people I am loth.
But if they rebel, they must go to hell:
They shall have a Priest & a passing bell.
muttering—
"Theyv caused all this trouble in the South. The 45
responsible blacks dont want to have anything to do
with them. Now they are making trouble here. But
theyv been arrested and fingerprinted; we know who
they are; we know how to stop them . . ."
Farted & belch'd & cough'd 50
And said, 'I love hanging & drawing & quartering
Every bit as well as war & slaughtering . . .'
(in his first campaign, Stevenson, facing the Korean abattoir:
"We will continue to pursue our peaceful purposes in Asia")
Damn praying & singing 55
Unless they will bring in
The blood of ten thousand by fighting or swinging
3) that only some three hundred students are concerned
about freedom of speech; only
thirty, the hard core [Kerr] 60
but behind them
a hidden community, three thousand
outside the university in this
conspiracy for free speech

This wave will retreat and men will cease to care . . . 65

Each day the last day; each day the
beginning the first word
door of the day or law awakening we create,
vowels such in a field in mid-morning
awakening the heart from its oppressions. 70

Evil "referrd to the root of *up, over*"
simulacra of law that wild over-rule
the Law man's inner nature seeks,
coils about them, not men but
heads and armors of the worm office is 75

There being no common good, no commune,
no communion, outside the freedom of
individual volition.

Gail Chiarrello (Dusenbery)

The Opening Session of Congress Rock and Roll

Wide across the plains . . burning grass; the buffalo of
Omaha;
Snow-capped peaks, the rank shoulders, dry rock,
glistening, scrub pines, dirt, the
massive boulders glinting in 5
the sun sulphur jetting
out of the earth,

Old Faithful, of Liberty, native sons of the earth, hoes, and
cards,
the Pinole Inn, hard drinks, roadhouses, cars in 10
Montana,

freedom sunburn sidewhiskers an old man with
a gold nugget in his
tooth old hands
old wood the
metal pan
for
washing gold
out of the earth; Indians
in ragged clothes, baskets of pine 20
bark and wampum from a longhouse in the east
shells

on lake Michigan, Ouisconsin, Minneapolis; strong-man,
he-man, hey,
skinny Charles Atlas; posing 25
brawn manifest, destiny
of will or buffalo
and plains;
wild men, their teeth
flashing in their mustaches, 30
two Colts hanging from their belts, and
a banjo, in the cave, an old
woman with a pail of water,

soup, or laundry, for
the revolutionary
Instant-Men
in her
bound by ages, rock, stalactite,
crystal secret hidden in her
den, mother, Bear-Mother, 40
berries for her young,
pawing honey hives in sun-light stones, mountains,
down the rocks, the rolling acres,
the boulders in the canyon,
free, stands erect, 45
American man.

TV and IBM, ICBM, ACLU, AACP, and CIO,
signals flashing in a storm
drenched union, nation,
plains, mountains, 50
eastern watershed, the lakes,
huge emptying basins
barges; teenage girls with pony tails
and white wool socks, and saddle shoes,
camped in the woods, girl scouts, 55
the Indian call; bone
whistle; blood beating
to the tomtoms in
the earth
they stand 60
on:
Girl Scouts
of the world, turn on,
grow pot, string beads, throw tents
open to your tramping kin, 65
kissing cousins,
weaving grass, the angels' hair,
baskets, games with high-
faluting titles:
secret initials, 70
the hood of closeness,
bonds in blood, same stock, same
family tree, poplar or
cottonwood waving on
the Iowa prairie, meadow larks, 75
the linden in New York; in Forest Hills the
sycamores, the tennis courts, the knowing youth

with scholarships to the great institution,
Government, until the President is
twelve years old, a native son, 80
a genius, Savio, Bob Dylan,
giving the beat to a
Congress that is
making
peace, 85
in
Latin
church American language
hip to the restive shadows of the
old, the ghosts, laid free to the wind the thread 90
across the spindle in its own
particular pattern, spin-
ning discs of plastic
sound or round or
square TV tubes 95
the opening
session
of
congress
rock-and-roll. 100

Bob Dylan

A Hard Rain's A-Gonna Fall

Where have you been my blue eyed son?
Where have you been my darlin' young one?
I've stumbled on the side of twelve misty mountains
I've walked and I've crawled on six crooked highways
I've stepped in the middle of seven sad forests 5
I've been out in front of a dozen dead oceans
I've been ten thousand miles in the mouth of a graveyard
And it's a hard, hard, hard, hard
And it's a hard rain's a gonna fall.

What did you see my blue eyed son? 10
What did you see my darlin' young one?
I saw a new born babe with wild wolves all around it;
I saw a highway of golden with nobody on it;
I saw a black branch with blood that kept dripping;
I saw a room full of men with their hammers a-bleeding; 15
I saw a white ladder all covered with water;
I saw ten thousand talkers whose tongues were all broken;
I saw guns and sharp swords in the hands of young children.
And it's a hard, hard, hard, hard,
And it's a hard rain's a gonna fall. 20

What did you hear my blue eyed son?
What did you hear my darlin' young one?
I heard the sound of a thunder that roared out a warning;
I heard the roar of a wave that could drown the whole world;
I heard one hundred drummers whose hands were a-blazing; 25
I heard ten thousand whispering and nobody listening
I heard one person starve, I heard many persons laughing;
I heard the song of a poet who died in the gutter,
I heard the sounds of a clown who cried in the alley;
I heard the sound of one person who cried he was human. 30
And it's a hard, hard, hard, hard,
And it's a hard rain's a gonna fall.

Who did you meet my blue eyed son?
Who did you meet my darlin' young one?
I met a young child beside a dead pony; 35
I met a white man who walked a black dog;
I met a young woman whose body was burning;
I met a young girl, she gave me a rainbow;
I met one man who was wounded in love;
I met another man who was wounded in hatred. 40
And it's a hard, hard, hard, hard,
And it's a hard rain's a gonna fall.

What'll you do now my blue eyed son?
What'll you do now my darlin' young one?
I'm a-going back out fore the rain starts a falling; 45
I'll walk to the depths of the deepest dark forest;
Where the people are many and their hands are all empty;
Where the pellets of poison are flooding their waters;
Where the home in the valley meets the damp dirty prison;
Where the executioner's face is always well hidden; 50
Where the hunger is ugly, where souls are forgotten;
Where black is the color, where none is the number;

And I'll tell it and speak it and think it and breathe it;
And reflect from the mountain so all souls can see it;
And I'll stand on the ocean until I start sinking; 55
And I'll know my song well before I start singing.
And it's a hard, hard, hard, hard,
And it's a hard rain's a gonna fall.

Bernard Lionel Einbond

A Happy Yellow Window Shade

In my dream you were a happy yellow window shade
And I a nervous pair of drapes;
You were pulled down and up
And I was drawn together and apart.
No curtain came between us,
Yet we never touched;
For I went in and out on a rod
And you went up and down on a roll;
And we were worked by separate cords.

Mari E. Evans

The Emancipation of George-Hector (a colored turtle)

George-Hector
. . . is
spoiled.
formerly he stayed
well up in his 5
shell . . . but now
he hangs arms and legs
sprawlingly
in a most languorous fashion . . .
head rared back 10
to
be admired.

he didn't use to talk . . .
but
he does now. 15

Mari E. Evans

The Rebel

When I
die
I'm sure
I will have a
Big Funeral . . . 5
Curiosity
seekers . . .
coming to see
if I
am really 10
Dead . . .
or just
trying to make
Trouble . . .

Lawrence Ferlinghetti

Assassination Raga

Tune in to a raga
on the stereo
and turn on Death TV
without its sound
Outside the plums are growing in a tree 5
'The force that through the green fuse
drives the flower'
drives Death TV
'A grief ago'
They lower the body soundlessly 10
into a huge plane in Dallas
into a huge plane in Los Angeles
marked 'United States of America'
and soundlessly
the 'United States of America' 15
takes off
& wings away with that Body
Tune out the TV sound
& listen soundlessly
to the blind mouths of its motors 20
& a sitar speaking on the stereo
a raga in a rage
at all that black death
and all that bad karma
La illaha el lill Allah 25
There is no god but God
The force that through the red fuze
drives the bullet
drives the needle in its dharma groove
and man the needle 30
drives that plane
of the 'United States of America'
through its sky full of shit & death
and the sky never ends
as it wings soundlessly 35
from those fucked-up cities

whose names we'd rather not remember
Inside the plane
inside the plane a wife
lies soundlessly 40
against the coffin
Engine whines as sitar signs outrageously
La illaha el lill Allah
There is no god but God?
There is no god but Death 45
The plums are falling through the tree
The force that drives the bullet
through the gun
drives everyone
as the 'United States of America' 50
flies on sightlessly
through the swift fierce years
with the dead weight of its Body
which they keep flying from Dallas
which they keep flying from Los Angeles 55
And the plane lands
without folding its wings
its shadow in mourning for itself
withdraws into itself
in death's draggy dominion 60
La illaha el lill Allah
There is no god but Death
The force that through the green fuze
drove his life
drives everyone 65
La illaha el lill Allah
And they are driving the Body
up Fifth Avenue
past a million people in line 70
'We are going to be here a long time'
says Death TV's spielman
The cortège passes soundlessly
'Goodbye! Goodbye!' some people cry
The traffic flows around & on 75
The force that drives the cars
combusts our karma
La illaha el lill Allah
There is no god but Death
The force that drives our life to death 80
drives sitar too
so soundlessly

La illaha el lill Allah
And they lift the Body
They lift the body 85
of the United States of America
and carry it into a cathedral
singing Hallelujah He Shall Live
For ever & ever
And then the Body moves again 90
down Fifth Avenue
Fifty-seven black sedans after it
There are people with roses
behind the barricades
in bargain-basement dresses 95
And sitar sings & sings nonviolence
sitar sounds in us its images of ecstasy
its depth of ecstasy
against old dung & death
La illaha el lill Allah 100
La illaha el lill Allah
The force that strikes its strings
strikes us
And the funeral train
the silver train 105
starts up soundlessly
at a dead speed
over the hot land
an armed helicopter over it
They are clearing the tracks ahead of assassins 110
The tracks are lined with bare faces
A highschool band in New Brunswick plays
The Battle Hymn of the Republic

They have shot it down again
They have shot him down again 115
& will shoot him down again
& take him on a train
& lower him again
into a grave in Washington
La illaha el lill Allah 120
Day & night journeys the coffin
through the dark land
too dark now to see the dark faces
La illaha el lill Allah
Plums & planes are falling through the air 125
La illaha el lill Allah
as sitar sings the only answer

sitar sings its only answer
sitar sounds the only sound
that still can still all violence 130
La illaha el lill Allah
There is no god but Life
Sitar says it Sitar sounds it
Sitar sounds on us to love love & hate hate
Sitar breathes its Atman breath in us 135
sounds & sounds in us its lovely *om om*
La illaha el lill Allah
At every step the pure wind rises
La illaha el lill Allah
People with roses
behind the barricades! 140

Lawrence Ferlinghetti

In a Surrealist Year

In a surrealist year
of sandwichmen and sunbathers
dead sunflowers and live telephones
house-broken politicos with party whips
performed as usual 5
in the rings of their sawdust circuses
where tumblers and human cannonballs
filled the air like cries
when some cool clown
pressed an inedible mushroom button 10
and an inaudible Sunday bomb
fell down
catching the president at his prayers
on the 19th green

O it was a spring 15
of fur leaves and cobalt flowers
when cadillacs fell thru the trees like rain
drowning the meadows with madness
while every imitation cloud
dropped myriad wingless crowds 20
of nutless nagasaki survivors

And lost teacups
full of our ashes
floated by

Lawrence Ferlinghetti

from Tyrannus Nix?

Nixon Nixon bush league President this is a
populist hymn to you and yours   And I begin
with your face and come back to your face
For 'our history is noble and tragic like
the mask of a tyrant'   And the mask   5
an actor wears is apt to become his face

Nixon Nixon I saw your childhood home on TV
I saw your childhood face   It was the same
face the face of adult America   the face we
chose for America the space-race face the   10
race face the face that sunk a thousand
sampans the face we all love in the Geritol
ads the face of the nation facing the nation
on color TV   the electronic burner that replaced
the log fire   the electric log the gas log in color   15
with antenna up the chimney log   We sit entranced
by the burning images on the grid in the bright
grate the flickering faces in the crucible whose
light-intensity we can turn up to suit whose ver-
tical image we can adjust so that the lower half   20
of your face matches the upper half of your
face   What a groovy invention   Just what we
needed Old   Blunderbuss Face old Circuit
Preacher face American Gothic Bold face
with Italic lips on the teleprinter . . .   25

. . . Richie oh Richie I seem to be developing a real
fondness for you in spite of your spots   Do
you love me   How I'd love to be cheek-by-jowl
with you Old Buddy   How I'd love to get you in my
encounter group and discuss inner space with you   30
and find out what's behind that hogjaw jughead
mask   We land on the moon's inscrutable face
while yours is just as inscrutable   Maybe you're part

Oriental maybe we could discuss Far out Eastern
arts or poetry   Who's your favorite poet John 35
Greenleaf Whittier   I am thinking maybe it's actually
possible to communicate with you   Wouldn't that be
an unexpected development   I am thinking maybe it's not
too late and not too early and I'm thinking maybe it's not
why you can't just Declare Peace   You can 40
do it if Allen Ginsberg can and you can make
it stick Old Sticky Dick   You could have grabbed the
mike right after Inauguration and blurted it out
right there and then   I hereby declare the end
of the War Against Youth   Think what a hero 45
you'd be with People   or do you think people are
a danger to the public . . .

. . . Nixon oh Nixon the leaves are green in Whittier
today but as every poet who has just discovered
the word ecology will tell you DDT is kill- 50
ing the pelicans and their eco-system is our
own Hudson River related to Hunters Point
and Colorado River emptied into Vietcong Delta
Zap those spooks and niggers won't win
Nixon Nixon Black Power's at bat and I sit in 55
the white bleachers eating crackerjack and reading
the whole newspaper column by column trying to
discover where you're really at   A hero with a
thousand faces none of which fit   Every head
has got you in it now   Old Swivelhead . . . 60

. . . Nixon oh Nixon I am not asking you to turn
and live with animals   I am not asking you to commune
with trees although 'What times are these when a conver-
sation about a tree is almost a crime because it contains
so many silences about so many crimes'   I'm not asking 65
you to squat and chant the Great Prajna Paravnita
Sutra although you might get high and learn Why
Rivers Run Only One Way   It's an oriental secret
which might give you a clue to the geo-politics of
Vietnam   I'm not asking you to displace your Secondhand 70
God   I'm not asking you to eat your figleaf   I'm
just asking if you actually believe you can serve
the people and the State at the same time or serve
liberty and authority at the same time or tell the truth
and lie with the same mouth . . . 75

. . . Nix on Nix the original Fighting Quaker with
your Wasp's nest on Plymouth Rock rigged
with Pioneer Era Guidelines in a Great
Leap Backward into a new union-military-industrial
Dark Ages with far-out multi-media scenes of mass 80
paranoia as in Hieronymus Bosch   death and sen-
suality wedded in buggering napalmed natives and/or
off-color students clitorises quivering in the ulti-
mate orgasm of death   I salute thee national
pilot of our destines in Air Force One   I salute 85
thee mass murderer by complicity   While there is a
strung-out soul in Santa Rita Prison I am not free
While there is a napalmed class I am of it   I
raise my middle finger to you smiling supporter of
benevolent imperial nationalism built upon political 90
falsehoods which still rule Washington DC   and which you
and every other politician + president including Kennedy
were too political not to inherit   Don't call me
on your red telephone   War is good business
Invest your son . . . 95

. . . O Nixon Nixon I've cycled through your America
and through my America   I have seen the faces
Let us now praise unfamous men   The People Yes
and No including Indian chiefs and tyrants queers
Kings hausfraus athletes parents policemen bosses 100
soldiers sex-offenders jewish newspapermen long-
haired students and Tuli Kupferberg   I see
we're all demented remnants of light and
ecstasy   Derelicts in time trying to reconstruct
with only faint recall a lost message Peace Music 105
Love Revolution Joy   This is the first day of the
rest of your life   This is your Safe Conduct Pass
There is Nothing to fear   For Nothing the only thing
to fear in a face   I've hitched back and
forth across the face of America looking for 110
a face   I once rode a freight from Joplin
to Chattanooga and saw your face on a siding
It was the face of the Yard Dick busting the
sterno bums   I was a college kid and
thought it was fun   The whole world a frater- 115
nity razing   But now I remember the face
in the dark by the tracks the dark jowls and
the hard eyes like yours oh American Dick   The
Eagle flies today brandishing olive branches and thunder-
bolts   Which will you drop on us . . . 120

Edward Field

Notes from a Slave Ship

It is necessary to wait until the boss's eyes are on you
Then simply put your work aside,
Slip a fresh piece of paper in the typewriter,
And start to write a poem.

Let their eyes boggle at your impudence; 5
The time for a poem is the moment of assertion,
The moment when you say I exist–
Nobody can buy my time absolutely.

Nobody can buy me even if I say, Yes I sell.
There I am sailing down the river, 10
Quite happy about the view of the passing towns,
When I find that I have jumped overboard.

There is always a long swim to freedom.
The worst of it is the terrible exhaustion
Alone in the water in the darkness, 15
The shore a fading memory and the direction lost.

Edward Field

A Bill to My Father

I am typing up bills for a firm to be sent to their clients.
It occurs to me that firms are sending bills to my father
Who has that way an identity I do not often realize.
He is a person who buys, owes, and pays,
Not papa like he is to me. 5
His creditors reproach him for not paying on time
With a bill marked "Please Remit."
I reproach him for never having shown his love for me
But only his disapproval.
He has a debt to me too 10
Although I have long since ceased asking him to come across;
He does not know how and so I do without it.
But in this impersonal world of business
He can be communicated with:
With absolute assurance of being paid 15
The boss writes "Send me my money"
And my father sends it.

Edward Field

The Statue of Liberty

All the ships are sailing away without me.
Day after day I hear their horns announcing
To the wage earners at their desks
That it is too late to get aboard.

They steam out of the harbor 5
With the statue of a French woman waving them good'by
Who used to be excellent to welcome people with
But is better lately for departures.

The French gave her to us as a reminder
Of their slogan and our creed 10
Which hasn't done much good
Because we have turned a perfectly good wilderness
Into a place nice to visit but not to live in.

Forever a prisoner in the harbor
On her star-shaped island of gray stones 15
She has turned moldy looking and shapeless
And her bronze drapery stands oddly into the wind.

From this prison-like island
I watch the ships sailing away without me
Disappearing one by one, day after day, 20
Into the unamerican distance,

And in my belly is one sentence: *Set Freedom Free,*
As the years fasten me into place and attitude,
Hand upraised and face into the wind
That no longer brings tears to my eyes. 25

Edward Field

Unwanted

The poster with my picture on it
Is hanging on the bulletin board in the Post Office.

I stand by it hoping to be recognized
Posing first full face and then profile

But everybody passes by and I have to admit 5
The photograph was taken some years ago.

I was unwanted then and I'm unwanted now
Ah guess ah'll go up echo mountain and crah.

I wish someone would find my fingerprints somewhere
Maybe on a corpse and say, You're it. 10

Description: Male, or reasonably so
White, but not lily-white and usually deep-red

Thirty-fivish, and looks it lately
Five-feet-nine and one-hundred-thirty pounds: no physique

Black hair going gray, hairline receding fast 15
What used to be curly, now fuzzy

Brown eyes starey under beetling brow
Mole on chin, probably will become a wen

It is perfectly obvious that he was not popular at school
No good at baseball, and wet his bed. 20

His aliases tell his history: Dumbell, Good-for-nothing,
Jewboy, Fieldinsky, Skinny, Fierce Face, Greaseball, Sissy.

Warning: This man is not dangerous, answers to any name
Responds to love, don't call him or he will come.

Donald Finkel

Give Way

Give way to the man coming at you:
He is probably organized, or he
Is a Mason, so much the worse
For you. The child ahead of you
Walks carefully, does not step 5
On a crack. She knows. Keep
Close to the buildings, stick
To the well-lit avenues, give way.

"Man that is born of woman is of
Few days, and full of trouble. 10
He cometh forth like a flower,
And is cut down: he fleeth also
As a shadow, and continueth not."
Your path will be covered with cracks;
Beware of a tall man who will bring 15
Ill fortune; beware of a short man:
He will be armed.

Or, better yet,
Organize, call meetings, make speeches,
Pay dues. With the dues, acquire 20
A public address system, and make
Louder speeches. Cast ballots, win.

If you will notice, now, the tall
Man, he tests the microphones,
The short man insures with his gun 25
The collection of dues; everyone
Is stepping between the cracks.
However, nobody is fully satisfied:
Keep close to the buildings, give way;
The man coming at you may be armed. 30

Robert Frost

Departmental

An ant on the tablecloth
Ran into a dormant moth
Of many times his size.
He showed not the least surprise.
His business wasn't with such. 5
He gave it scarcely a touch,
And it was off on his duty run.
Yet if he encountered one
Of the hive's enquiry squad
Whose work is to find out God 10
And the nature of time and space,
He would put him onto the case.
Ants are a curious race;
One crossing with hurried tread
The body of one of their dead 15
Isn't given a moment's arrest—
Seems not even impressed.
But he no doubt reports to any
With whom he crosses antennae,
And they no doubt report 20
To the higher up at court.
Then word goes forth in Formic:
"Death's come to Jerry McCormic,
Our selfless forager Jerry.
Will the special Janizary 25
Whose office it is to bury
The dead of the commissary
Go bring him home to his people.
Lay him in state on a sepal.
Wrap him for shroud in a petal. 30
Embalm him with ichor of nettle.
This is the word of your Queen."
And presently on the scene
Appears a solemn mortician;
And taking formal position 35
With feelers calmly atwiddle.

Seizes the dead by the middle,
And heaving him high in air,
Carries him out of there.
No one stands round to stare. 40
It is nobody else's affair.

It wouldn't be called ungentle.
But how thoroughly departmental.

Allen Ginsberg

Death to Van Gogh's Ear!

POET is Priest
Money has reckoned the soul of America
Congress broken thru to the precipice of Eternity
the President built a War machine which will vomit and rear up
Russia out of Kansas 5
The American Century betrayed by a mad Senate which no
longer sleeps with its wife
Franco has murdered Lorca the fairy son of Whitman
just as Mayakovsky committed suicide to avoid Russia
Hart Crane distinguished Platonist committed suicide to cave in 10
the wrong America
just as millions of tons of human wheat were burned in secret
caverns under the White House
while India starved and screamed and ate mad dogs full of rain
and mountains of eggs were reduced to white powder in the halls 15
of Congress
no godfearing man will walk there again because of the stink of
the rotten eggs of America
and the Indians of Chiapas continue to gnaw their vitaminless
tortillas 20
aborigines of Australia perhaps gibber in the eggless wilderness
and I rarely have an egg for breakfast tho my work requires
infinite eggs to come to birth in Eternity
eggs should be eaten or given to their mothers
and the grief of the countless chickens of America is expressed 25
in the screaming of her comedians over the radio
Detroit has built a million automobiles of rubber trees and
phantoms
but a walk, I walk, and the Orient walks with me, and all Africa
walks 30
and sooner or later North America will walk
for as we have driven the Chinese Angel from our door he will
drive us from the Golden Door of the future
we have not cherished pity on Tanganyika
Einstein alive was mocked for his heavenly politics 35

Bertrand Russell driven from New York for getting laid
and the immortal Chaplin has been driven from our shores with
    the rose in his teeth
a secret conspiracy by Catholic Church in the lavatories of
    Congress has denied contraceptives to the unceasing   40
    masses of India.
Nobody publishes a word that is not the cowardly robot ravings
    of a depraved mentality
the day of the publication of the true literature of the American
    body will be day of Revolution   45
the revolution of the sexy lamb
the only bloodless revolution that gives away corn
poor Genet will illuminate the harvesters of Ohio
Marijuana is a benevolent narcotic but J. Edgar Hoover prefers
    his deathly scotch   50
And the heroin of Lao-Tze & the Sixth Patriarch is punished
    by the electric chair
but the poor sick junkies have nowhere to lay their heads
fiends in our government have invented a cold-turkey cure for
    addiction as obsolete as the Defense Early Warning Radar   55
    System
I am the defense early warning radar system
I see nothing but bombs
I am not interested in preventing Asia from being Asia
and the governments of Russia and Asia will rise and fall but   60
    Asia and Russia will not fall
the government of America also will fall but how can America
    fall
I doubt if anyone will fall anymore except governments
fortunately all the governments will fall   65
the only ones which won't fall are the good ones
and the good ones don't yet exist
But they have to begin existing they exist in my poems
they exist in the death of the Russian and American governments
they exist in the death of Hart Crane & Mayakovsky   70
Now is the time for prophecy without death as a consequence
the universe will ultimately disappear
Hollywood will rot on the windmills of Eternity
Hollywood whose movies stick in the throat of God
Yes Hollywood will get what it deserves   75
Time
Seepage or nerve-gas over the radio
History will make this poem prophetic and its awful silliness a
    hideous spiritual music

I have the moan of doves and the feather of ecstacy 80
Man cannot long endure the hunger of the cannibal abstract
War is abstract
the world will be destroyed
but I will die only for poetry, that will save the world
Monument to Sacco & Vanzetti not yet financed to ennoble 85
Boston
natives of Kenya tormented by idiot con-men from England
South Africa in the grip of the white fool
Vachel Lindsay Secretary of the Interior
Poe Secretary of Imagination 90
Pound Secty. Economics
and Kra belongs to Kra, and Pukti to Pukti
crossfertilization of Blok and Artaud
Van Gogh's Ear on the currency
no more propaganda for monsters 95
and poets should stay out of politics or become monsters
I have become monsterous with politics
the Russian poet undoubtedly monsterous in his secret notebook
Tibet should be left alone
These are obvious prophecies 100
America will be destroyed
Russian poets will struggle with Russia
Whitman warned against this 'fabled Damned of nations'
Where was Theodore Roosevelt when he sent out ultimatums
from his castle in Camden 105
Where was the House of Representatives when Crane read aloud
from his prophetic books
What was Wall Street scheming when Lindsay announced the
doom of Money
Were they listening to my ravings in the locker rooms of Bick- 110
fords Employment Offices?
Did they bend their ears to the moans of my soul when I
struggled with market research statistics in the Forum at
Rome?
No they were fighting in fiery offices, on carpets of heartfailure, 115
screaming and bargaining with Destiny
fighting the Skeleton with sabres, muskets, buck teeth, indigestion,
bombs of larceny, whoredom, rockets, pederasty,
back to the wall to build up their wives and apartments, lawns,
suburbs, fairydoms, 120
Puerto Ricans crowded for massacre on 114th St. for the sake
of an imitation Chinese-Moderne refrigerator
Elephants of mercy murdered for the sake of an Elizabethan
birdcage

millions of agitated fanatics in the bughouse for the sake of the screaming soprano of industry 125

Money-chant of soapers—toothpaste apes in television sets—deodorizers on hypnotic chairs—

petroleum mongers in Texas—jet plane streaks among the clouds— 130

sky writers liars in the face of Divinity—fanged butchers of hats and shoes, all Owners! Owners! Owners! with obsession on property and vanishing Selfhood!

and their long editorials on the fence of the screaming negro attacked by ants crawled out of the front page! 135

Machinery of a mass electrical dream! A war-creating Whore of Babylon bellowing over Capitols and Academies!

Money! Money! Money! shrieking mad celestial money of illusion! Money made of nothing, starvation, suicide! Money of failure! Money of death! 140

Money against Eternity! and eternity's strong mills grind out vast paper of illusion!

John Haines

And When the Green Man Comes

The man is clothed
in birchbark,
small birds cling to his limbs
and one builds
a nest in his ear. 5

The clamor of bedlam
infests his hair, a wind
blowing in his head
shakes down
a thought that turns 10
to moss and lichen
at his feet.

His eyes are blind
with April,
his breath distilled 15
of butterflies
and bees, and in his beard
the maggot sings.

He comes again
with litter of chips 20
and empty cans,
his shoes full of mud and dung;

an army of shedding dogs
attends him,
the valley shudders where 25
he stands,
                redolent of roses,
exalted in
the streaming rain.

John Haines

Divided, the Man Is Dreaming

One half
lives in sunlight; he is
the hunter and calls
the beasts of the field
about him. 5
Bathed in sweat and tumult
he slakes and kills,
eats meat
and knows blood.

His other half 10
lies in shadow
and longs for stillness,
a corner of the evening
where birds
rest from flight: 15
cool grass grows at his feet,
dark mice feed
from his hands.

John Haines

Horns

I went to the edge of the wood
in the color of evening,
and rubbed with a piece of horn
against a tree,
believing the great, dark moose 5
would come, his eyes
on fire with the moon.

I fell asleep in an old white tent,
the October moon rose,
and down a wide, frozen stream 10
the moose came roaring,
hoarse with rage and desire.

I awoke and stood in the cold
as he slowly circled the camp.
His horns exploded in the brush 15
with dry trees cracking
and falling, his nostrils flared
as, swollen-necked, smelling
of challenge, he stalked by me.

I called him back, and he came 20
and stood in the shadow
not far away, and gently rubbed
his horns against the icy willows.
I heard him breathing softly.
Then with a faint sigh of warning 25
soundlessly he walked away.

I stood there in the moonlight,
and the darkness and silence
surged back, flowing around me,
full of a wild enchantment, 30
as though a god had spoken.

John Haines

Poem

The immense sadness
of approaching winter
hangs in the air
this cloudy September.

Today a muddy road 5
filled with leaves, tomorrow
the stiffening earth and
a footprint
glazed with ice.

The sun breaking through 10
still warm, but the road
deep in shadow;
your hand in mine is cold.

Our berries picked,
the mushrooms gathered, 15
each of us hides
in his heart a small piece
of this summer,
as mice store their roots
in a place 20
known only to them.

We believe in the life to come,
when the stark tree
stands in silence above
the blackened leaf; 25
but now at a bend in the road
to stop and listen:

strange song
of a southbound bird
overflows 30
in the quiet dusk
from the top
of that tree.

John Haines

The Great Society

Having been whipped through Paradise
and seen humanity
strolling like an overfed beast
set loose from its cage,
a man may long for nothing so much
as a house of snow,
a blue stone for a lamp,
and a skin to cover his head.

John Haines

The Mole

Sometimes I envy those
who spring like great black-
and-gold butterflies
before the crowded feet
of summer— 5
brief, intense,
like pieces of the sun,
they are remembered and celebrated
long after night has fallen.

But I believe also in one 10
who in the dead of winter
tunnels through a damp,
clinging darkness,
nosing the soil of old gardens.

He lives unnoticed, but 15
deep within him there is a dream
of the surface one day
breaking and crumbling:

and a small, brown-furred
figure stands there, 20
blinking at the sky,
as the rising sun slowly dries
his strange, unruly wings.

Anthony Hecht

Black Boy in the Dark

Peace, tawny slave, half me and half thy dam!
Did not thy hue bewray whose brat thou art,
. . .
Villain, thou mightst have been an emperor.
—Titus Andronicus

Summer. A hot, moth-populated night.
Yesterday's maples in the village park
Are boxed away into the vaults of dark,
To be returned tomorrow, like our flag,
Which was brought down from its post office height 5
At sunset, folded, and dumped in a mailbag.

Wisdom, our Roman matron, perched on her throne
In front of the library, the Civil war
Memorial (History and Hope) no more
Are braced, trustworthy figures. Some witching skill 10
Softly dismantled them, stone by heavy stone,
And the small town, like Bethlehem, lies still.

And it is still at the all-night service station,
Where Andy Warhol's primary colors shine
In simple commercial glory, the Esso sign 15
Revolving like a funland lighthouse, where
An eighteen-year-old black boy clocks the nation,
Reading a comic book in a busted chair.

Our solitary guardian of the law
Of diminishing returns? The President, 20
Addressing the first contingent of draftees sent
To Viet Nam, was brief: "Life is not fair,"
He said, and was right, of course. Everyone saw
What happened to him in Dallas. We were there,

We suffered, we were Whitman. And now the boy 25
Daydreams about the White House, the rising shares
Of Standard Oil, the whited sepulchres.
But what, after all, has he to complain about,
This expendable St. Michael we employ
To stay away and keep the darkness out? 30

David Hilton

In Praise of BIC Pens

Others always skip over the word
That will bring the belligerents of the world
To the negotiating table, if only

I can get it written, or will
Teach thin kids in Woetown, West Virginia, 5
To rebound tough and read Ted Roethke—

I'm writing along in a conspiracy
of birds and sun and pom-pom girls
Lines to cheer old ladies with shopping bags

Waiting by their busstops at 5PM 10
Or lines to get the 12-years-olds off cigarettes
Or save the suicides in gay-bar mensrooms

Or save the fat man from his refrigerator
Or the brilliant boy from color TV
Or the RA private from re-upping for six 15

Or the whole Midwest from wanting to conquer Asia and
the Moon
Or the current president from his place in history—
Oh, if only I can get it written

No one will burn kittens or slap little boys or make little girls 20
cry
Or cower at cancer or coronaries or plain palsied old age
Or get goofy from radiation in his cornflake milk—

If only I can get it written. But always
When I get close to the word and the crowd begins to roar 25
The common pen skips, leaves the page blank—

But you, BIC pen, at nineteen cents, could trace truce terms
on tank treads,

Could ratify in the most flourishing script
The amnesty of love for our most dreaded enemies: 30

The ugly, the poor, the stupid, the sexually screwed-up—
Etching their releases across the slippery communiqués of
generals and governors,
For Behold you can write upon butter, Yea inscribe even
through slime! 35

But at nineteen cents no one pays attention
To the deadwood you shatter or the manifestoes you slice in
the ice—
For who would believe Truth at *that* price.

Frank Horne

Kid Stuff

December, 1942

The wise guys
tell me
that Christmas
is Kid Stuff . . .
Maybe they've got 5
something there—
Two thousand years ago
three wise guys
chased a star
across a continent 10
to bring
frankincense and myrrh
to a Kid
born in a manger
with an idea in his head . . . 15

And as the bombs
crash
all over the world
today
the real wise guys 20
know
that we've all
got to go chasing stars
again
in the hope 25
that we can get back
some of that
Kid Stuff
born two thousand years ago.

Colette Inez

Slumnight

T.V. gunning down
the hours
serves as sheriff
in a room
where one yawn 5
triggers off another,

sends time scuffling
into night.
Wars slugged out
on vacant lots 10
sign an armistice
with sleep.

Turned to a wall,
the children dream
and the moon pulls up 15
in a squadcar.

LeRoi Jones

For Hettie

My wife is left-handed.
which implies a fierce de-
termination. A complete other
worldliness. IT'S WEIRD, BABY.
The way some folks 5
are always trying to be
different. A sin & a shame.
But then, she's been a bohemian
all of her life . . . black stockings
refusing to take orders. I sit 10
patiently, trying to tell her
whats right. TAKE THAT DAMN
PENCIL OUTTA THAT HAND. YOU'RE
RITING BACKWARDS. & such. but
to no avail. & it shows 15
in her work. Left-handed coffee,
Left-handed eggs; when she comes
in at night . . . it's her left hand
offered for me to kiss. Damn.
& now her belly droops over the seat. 20
They say it's a child. But
I ain't quite so sure.

Galway Kinnell

from The Avenue Bearing the Initial of Christ into the New World

1

pcheeck   pcheek   pcheek   pcheek   pcheek
They cry. The motherbirds thieve the air
To appease them. A tug on the East River
Blasts the bass-note of its passage, lifted
from the infra-bass of the sea. A broom   5
Swishes over the sidewalk like feet through leaves.
Valerio's pushcart Ice Coal Kerosene
Moves   clack
                    clack
                              clack   10
On a broken wheelrim.   Ringing in its chains
The New Star Laundry horse comes down the street
Like a roofleak whucking in a pail.
At the redlight, where a horn blares,
The Golden Harvest Bakery brakes on its gears,   15
Squeaks, and seethes in place.   A propane-
gassed bus makes its way with big, airy sighs.

Across the street a woman throws open
Her window,
She sets, terribly softly,   20
Two potted plants on the windowledge
          tic   tic
And bangs shut her window.

A man leaves a doorway tic toc tic toc tic toc tic hurrah
   toc splat on Avenue C tic etc and turns the corner.   25

Banking the same corner
A pigeon coasts 5th Street in shadows.
Looks for altitude, surmounts the rims of buildings,
And turns white.

The babybirds pipe down.   It is day.   30

3

From the Station House
Under demolishment on Houston
To the Power Station on 14th,
Jews, Negroes, Puerto Ricans
Walk in the spring sunlight. 35

The Downtown Talmud Torah
Blosztein's Cutrate Bakery
Areceba Panataria Hispano
Peanuts Dried Fruit Nuts & Canned Goods
Productos Tropicales 40
Appetizing Herring Candies Nuts
Nathan Kugler Chicken Store Fresh Killed Daily
Little Rose Restaurant
Rubinstein the Hatter Mens Boys Hats Caps Furnishings
J. Herrmann Dealer in All Kinds of Bottles 45
Natural Bloom Cigars
Blony Bubblegum
Mueren las Cucarachas Super Potente Garantizada de Matar las
        Cucarachas mas Resistentes
Wenig מצבות
G. Schnee Stairbuilder 50
Everyouth la Original Loción Eterna Juventud Satisfacción Dinero
        Devuelto
Happy Days Bar & Grill

Through dust-stained windows over storefronts
Curtains drawn aside, onto the Avenue
Thronged with Puerto Ricans, Negroes, Jews, 55
Baby carriages stuffed with groceries and babies,
The old women peer, blessed damozels
Sitting up there forever in the cockroached rooms,
Eating fresh-killed chicken, productos tropicales,
Appetizing herring, canned goods, nuts; 60
They puff out smoke from Natural Bloom cigars
And one day they puff like Blony Bubblegum.
Across the square skies with faces in them
Pigeons skid, crashing into the brick.
From a rooftop a boy fishes at the sky. 65
Around him a flock of pigeons fountains,
Blown down and swirling up again, seeking the sky.
From a skyview of the city they must seem
A whirlwind on the desert seeking itself;

Here they break from the rims of the buildings 70
Without rank in the blue military cemetery sky.
A red kite wriggles like a tadpole
Into the sky beyond them, crosses
The sun, lays bare its own crossed skeleton.
To fly from this place—to roll 80
On some bubbly blacktop in the summer,
To run under the rain of pigeon plumes, to be
Tarred, and feathered with birdshit, Icarus,

In Kugler's glass headdown dangling by yellow legs.

6

In the pushcart market, on Sunday, 85
A crate of lemons discharges light like a battery.
Icicle-shaped carrots that through black soil
Wove away like flames in the sun.
Onions with their shirts ripped seek sunlight
On green skins. The sun beats 90
On beets dirty as boulders in cowfields,
On turnips pinched and gibbous
From budging rocks, on embery sweets,
Peanut-shaped Idahos, shore-pebble Long Islands and Maines,
On horseradishes still growing weeds on the flat ends, 95
Cabbages lying about like sea-green brains
The skulls have been shucked from,
On tomatoes, undented plum-tomatoes, alligator skinned
Cucumbers, that float pickled
In the wooden tubs of green skim milk— 100

Sky-flowers, dirt-flowers, underdirt-flowers,
Those that climbed for the sun in their lives
And those that wormed away—equally uprooted,
Maimed, lopped, shucked, and misaimed.

In the market in Damascus a goat 105
Came to a stall where twelve goatheads
Were lined up for sale. It sniffed them
One by one. Finally thirteen goats started
Smiling in their faintly sardonic way.

A crone buys a pickle from a crone, 110
It is wrapped in the *Mirror*,
At home she will open the wrapping, stained,

And stare and stare and stare at it.
And the cucumbers, and the melons,
And the leeks, and the onions, and the garlic. 115

14

Behind the Power Station on 14th, the held breath
Of light, as God is a held breath, withheld,
Spreads the East River, into which fishes leak:
The brown sink or dissolve,
The white float out in shoals and armadas, 120
Even the gulls pass them up, pale
Bloated socks of riverwater and rotted seed,
That swirl on the tide, punched back
To the Hell Gate narrows, and on the ebb
Steam seaward, seeding the sea. 125

On the Avenue, through air tinted crimson
By neon over the bars, the rain is falling.
You stood once on Houston, among panhandlers and winos
Who weave the eastern ranges, learning to be free,
To not care, to be knocked flat and to get up clear-headed 130
Spitting the curses out. "Now be nice,"
The proprietor threatens; "Be nice," he cajoles.
"Fuck you," the bum shouts as he is hoisted again,
"God fuck your mother." (In the empty doorway,
Hunched on the empty crate, the crone gives no sign.) 135

That night a wildcat cab whined crosstown on 7th.
You knew even the traffic lights were made by God,
The red splashes growing dimmer the farther away
You looked, and away up at 14th, a few green stars;
And without sequence, and nearly all at once, 140
The red lights blinked into green,
And just before there was one complete Avenue of green,
The little green stars in the distance blinked.

It is night, and raining. You look down
Towards Houston in the rain, the living streets, 145
Where instants of transcendence
Drift in oceans of loathing and fear, like lanternfishes,
Or phosphorus flashings in the sea, or the feverish light
Skin is said to give off when the swimmer drowns at night.

From the blind gut Pitt to the East River of Fishes, 150
The Avenue cobbles a swath through the discolored air,

A roadway of refuse from the teeming shores and ghettos
And the Caribbean Paradise, into the new ghetto and new paradise,
This God-forsaken Avenue bearing the initial of Christ
Through the haste and carelessness of the ages, 155
The sea standing in heaps, which keeps on collapsing,
Where the drowned suffer a C-change,
And remain the common poor.

Since Providence, for the realization of some unknown purpose, has

seen fit to leave this dangerous people on the face of the earth, 160

and did not destroy it . . .

Listen! the swish of the blood,
The sirens down the bloodpaths of the night,
Bone tapping on the bone, nerve-nets
Singing under the breath of sleep– 165
We scattered over the lonely seaways,
Over the lonely deserts did we run,
In dark lanes and alleys did we hide ourselves . . .

The heart beats without windows in its night,
The lungs put out the light of the world as they 170
Heave and collapse, the brain turns and rattles
In its own black axlegrease–

In the nighttime
Of the blood they are laughing and saying,
Our little lane, what a kingdom it was! 175
oi weih, oi weih

Stanley Kunitz

The War against the Trees

The man who sold his lawn to standard oil
Joked with his neighbors come to watch the show
While the bulldozers, drunk with gasoline,
Tested the virtue of the soil
Under the branchy sky 5
By overthrowing first the privet-row.

Forsythia-forays and hydrangea-raids
Were but preliminaries to a war
Against the great-grandfathers of the town,
So freshly lopped and maimed. 10
They struck and struck again,
And with each elm a century went down.

All day the hireling engines charged the trees,
Subverting them by hacking underground
In grub-dominions, where dark summer's mole 15
Rampages through his halls,
Till a northern seizure shook
Those crowns, forcing the giants to their knees.

I saw the ghosts of children at their games
Racing beyond their childhood in the shade, 20
And while the green world turned its death-foxed page
And a red wagon wheeled,
I watched them disappear
Into the suburbs of their grievous age.

Ripped from the craters much too big for hearts 25
The club-roots bared their amputated coils,
Raw gorgons matted blind, whose pocks and scars
Cried Moon! on a corner lot
One witness-moment, caught
In the rear-view mirrors of the passing cars. 30

Carl Larsen

The Plot to Assassinate the Chase Manhattan Bank

To assassinate the Chase Manhattan Bank
Is not as easy as you'd think.
I walked in, see, and yelled "Kings-X!"
and saw what looked like great machines
come rumbling to a halt, and I thought, 5
fine—I'm halfway home. Then God rose from
the Office of the President,
a little miffed, I think, and said,
"What's on your mind?"
"I came up from the Coast," I said, 10
"to blow this pad to—if you will
excuse my pun—to Kingdom Come."
"You can't do that, my Son," he said,
and that's how I knew he was God,
although he looked a great deal 15
like John Wayne. "You wouldn't want,"
he said, "to do away with this—"
and from each teller's cage, a flock
of rainbow doves flew up, and settled
near the roof. "Put down your bomb, 20
let's have a talk," he said, and smiled.
I laid aside the bomb and followed him
into his office, and sat down.
"The Proletariat demands," I said,
"You cease this madness"; And he 25
smiled again. I saw he had a golden tooth.
"Some for the glories of this world,"
God said, then showed a picture of his family,
and then his house, a nice split-level
place up in the Bronx. His wife, 30
a pleasant-looking woman,
had inscribed it: "Love, In God We Trust."
He wiped away the tears that gathered
in the corners of his steely eyes,
choked back a sob, and called The Fuzz. 35
Inside a minute, forty cops popped from

the walls and drawers, came running from
the vault where God kept love, and
clamped the irons around my feet.
"Now Jean Valjean," God shouted, 40
gaining his composure, "now you'll
face the rack!" I pleaded it was all
a joke. I said I'd be a good li'l boy
and stay home playing with my spiders
if he'd let me go. But his bit was not 45
forgiveness, and they locked me in
a dungeon full of nasty things he had
discarded, like the stars,
and sea-foam, and the earth.

Denise Levertov

Merritt Parkway

As if it were
forever that they move, that we
keep moving—

Under a wan sky where
as the lights went on a star 5
pierced the haze and now
follows steadily
a constant
above our six lanes
the dreamlike continuum . . . 10

And the people—ourselves!
the humans from inside the
cars, apparent
only at gasoline stops
unsure, 15
eyeing each other

drink coffee hastily at the
slot machines and hurry
back to the cars
vanish 20
into them forever, to
keep moving—

Houses now and then beyond the
sealed road, the trees/trees, bushes
passing by, passing 25
the cars that
keep moving ahead of

us, past us, pressing behind us
and
over left, those that come 30
toward us shining too brightly
moving relentlessly

in six lanes, gliding
north and south, speeding with
a slurred sound— 35

Denise Levertov

What Were They like?

(*Questions and Answers*)

1) Did the people of Viet Nam
use lanterns of stone?
2) Did they hold ceremonies
to reverence the opening of buds?
3) Were they inclined to rippling laughter?
4) Did they use bone and ivory,
jade and silver, for ornament?
5) Had they an epic poem?
6) Did they distinguish between speech and singing?

1) Sir, their light hearts turned to stone.
It is not remembered whether in gardens
stone lanterns illumined pleasant ways.
2) Perhaps they gathered once to delight in blossom,
but after the children were killed
there were no more buds.
3) Sir, laughter is bitter to the burned mouth.
4) A dream ago, perhaps. Ornament is for joy.
All the bones were charred.
5) It is not remembered. Remember,
most were peasants; their life
was in rice and bamboo.
When peaceful clouds were reflected in the paddies
and the water-buffalo stepped surely along terraces,
maybe fathers told their sons old tales.
When bombs smashed the mirrors
there was time only to scream.
6) There is an echo yet, it is said,
of their speech which was like a song.
It is reported their singing resembled
the flight of moths in moonlight.
Who can say? It is silent now.

Robert Lowell

The Mouth of the Hudson

A single man stands like a bird-watcher,
and scuffles the pepper and salt snow
from a discarded, gray
Westinghouse Electric cable drum.
He cannot discover America by counting 5
the chains of condemned freight-trains
from thirty states. They jolt and jar
and junk in the siding below him.
He has trouble with his balance.
His eyes drop, 10
and he drifts with the wild ice
ticking seaward down the Hudson,
like the blank sides of a jig-saw puzzle.

The ice ticks seaward like a clock.
A Negro toasts 15
wheat-seeds over the coke-fumes
of a punctured barrel.
Chemical air
sweeps in from New Jersey,
and smells of coffee. 20

Across the river
ledges of suburban factories tan
in the sulphur-yellow sun
of the unforgivable landscape.

Walter Lowenfels

American Voices (II)

Across Jersey sand barrens
night is cradled in the arms of pine branches,
peach blossoms are shaking on the bough.
A jet plane from Pomona Air Base
zips its star across our sky, 5
but the ground of liberty is still gained by inches.

My name is Larry. My letter appeared in the
Wayne University Collegian, Detroit, Michigan:
"The world is not Americo-centric, and we are
participants in a world community, not masters 10
of it."

In South Jersey
across the Land of Lenapes
the deer trail is hidden in the cedar swamps,
cranberry pippins edge out of their moss. 15
In Bridgeton
a wife longs by her window:

Your ring warms my finger but you
have gone to the neighborhood of death.
I am washing the powder from my face 20
the lipstick from my lips.
When can we both lean by the wind-blown
curtains
and see the tears dry on each other's face?

In South Jersey 25
the wild laurel breathes over our tomato patches.
A pine wind dusts our hands and faces—
a farmer turns in his sleep wondering—
will morning bring radium or rain?
In a room in Vineland 30
a mother is parting from her son.
She cries but no sound breaks from her voice.
She clutches at him though her arms are still.
Who hears her song:

On the gray birches the moon shines cold. 35
Soon it will be warm in the woods of South Jersey.
When will my son return?
He was always a man of peace
and played baseball in the spring.

In South Jersey 40
whippoorwill calls sharpen our ears,
blueberry bushes wave through the dark
and peach blossoms send out perfume.
to make a peace treaty with spring.

My name is Marion. I wrote to the editor 45
of the Plain Dealer, Cleveland, Ohio:
"I can't help but shudder when the word
cobalt no longer describes the shade of blue but
conveys the idea of uncontrolled destruction."

In South Jersey 50
the sun is marching north
15 miles a day.
The tips of our scrub oaks are separating
into pink threads. Swamp magnolias
are crackling with light. 55
In Mays Landing
a girl reads her sweetheart's letter . . .

March, march, march
separated by 10,000 miles,
each in our corner. 60
The road is so far,
When shall we meet?
What is left us
but wanting to be together?
A copper coin or a stone 65
outlives any of us.
Only a good name endures.
We are all brothers,
each a branch from the same tree . . .
If I live I shall return, 70
if I do not,
we shall live in each other
forever.

I am Margaret. My letter was in the Free
Press, Detroit, Michigan. 75

"I will shortly become a mother for the first time, and this more than any single factor dramatizes to me the need for world peace."

In South Jersey
We do not yearn for the cedars of Lebanon. 80
At dawn we drink the alarm clock blues.
At dusk we eat the petals from our days.
We grieve over endless hungry children.
We mark down carefully how much we can endure.
We grind the tractor on the side of the sun, 85
flick the sky's face with an oak leaf,
order the bridge keeper at Somers Point—
OPEN UP!

Over Brigantine we look at the sky.
The rainbow we planted has arrived. 90
Our sunlight is already
bending across the mountain of today.
We are here!

Walter Lowenfels

The Great Peace

(from the Amerindian)

What is more beautiful
    than the land that has no grave
        because there is no fear,
where bravery doesn't bleed
        because there is no enemy,   5

where the warriors of the Hundred and One Nations
    uproot the tallest pine tree
and in the hole that's left
    drop their bombs and guns,

deep in the underearth,   10
    throw all their weapons,
and plant again the tree. Then
    when the Great Peace is won

we will find the land
    where truth is without a name   15
because there is no lie
    where charity has no home;
because there is no hunger;
    where nobody is an Unknown
Hero any more,   20
    and no one is a seer—
because the light of wisdom
    is everywhere.

Alastair Macdonald

T.V. News

Through the blind eye, groomed and deodorized,
expression in place for the cameras,
the news-reader nightly conjures
youth's protest against itself,
the violence of peace marches. 5

Confessional tones, remoter than insult,
impersonal concern virulent as sadism
(and he no doubt the best of men)
materialize the nude child ballooning with hunger,
the war victim terrorized, mangled, and shot. 10

They do not quite pass into the room.
Our nerves reject them, flick, while the image flicks
as if it had not been, to sweeter things:
nature, evocative dreams, the race's
idealisms, and averted wrongs. 15

But they are glimpsed, and root unquiet seeds.
Coexistent misery shares our tended calm;
implants a need to live this horror too
or be apart, impaired in the look for what
holds incompatible scenes in meaningful view. 20

Eugene McCarthy

Ares

god, Ares
is not dead.
he lives,
where blood and water mix
in tropic rains. 5
no NNE, or S
or W, no compass—
only mad roosters
tail down on twisted vanes
point to the wind 10
of the falling sky
the helicopter wind
that blows straight down
flattening the elephant grass
to show small bodies crawling 15
at the roots, or dead
and larger ones
in the edged shade, to be counted
for the pentagon, and
for the New York Times. 20

Ideologies can make a war,
last long and go far
Ideologies do not have boundaries
cannot be shown on maps,
before and after, 25
or even on a globe,
as meridian, parallel,
or papal line of demarcation.

What is the line between
Moslem and Jew 30
Christian and Infidel
Catholic and Huguenot
with St. Bartholomew waiting
on the calendar for his day

to come and go? 35
What map can choose between cropped heads
and hairy ones?
What globe affirm
"better dead than red"
"better red than dead"? 40
ideologies do not bleed
they only blood the world.

Mathematical wars go farther.
They run on ratios
of kill and overkill 45
from one to x
and to infinity.
We are bigger, one to two
We are better, one to three
Death is the measure 50
It's one of us to four
of them, or eight to two
depending on your
point of view.
12 to 3 55
means victory
12 to 5
forebodes defeat.
These ratios stand
sustained 60
by haruspex and IBM.
We can kill all of you
three times
and you kill all of us
but once and a half— the game 65
is prisoner's base, and we
are fresh on you
with new technology.
We sleep well
but worry some. We know 70
that you would kill us twice
if you could, and not leave
that second death half done.
we are unsure
that even three times killed 75
you might not spring up whole.
Snakes close again
and cats, do, it is true,

have nine lives. Why
not the same for you? 80
No one knows about third comings
We all wait for the second, which
may be bypassed
in the new arithmetic.
or which, when it comes, 85
may look like a first
and be denied.
The best war, if war must be,
is one for Helen
or for Aquitaine 90
No computation stands
and all the programed lights
flash
and burn slowly down to dark

when one man says 95
I will die,
not twice, or three times over
but my one first life, and last,
lay down for this my space,
my place, my love. 100

Eugene McCarthy

Three Bad Signs

The first Bad Sign is this:
"Green River Ordinance Enforced Here.
Peddlers Not Allowed."

This is a clean, safe town.
No one can just come round 5
With ribbons and bright threads
Or new books to be read.
This is an established place.
We have accepted patterns in lace,
And ban itinerant vendors of new forms 10
and whirls,
All things that turn the heads of girls.
We are not narrow, but we live with care.
Gypsies, hawkers and minstrels are right
for a fair. 15
But transient peddlers, nuisances, we say
From Green River must be kept away.
Traveling preachers, actors with a play,
Can pass through, but may not stay.
Phoenicians, Jews, men of Venice— 20
Know that this is the home of Kiwanis.
All of you who have been round the world
to find
Beauty in small things: read our sign
And move on. 25

The second Bad Sign is this:
"Mixed Drinks."

"Mixed Drinks."
What mystery blinks
As in the thin blood of the neon sign 30
The uncertain hearts of the customers
Are tested there in the window.
Embolism after embolism, repeating.

Mixed drinks between the art movie
And the Reasonable Rates Hotel. 35
Mixed drinks are class,
Each requires a different glass.
Mixed drink is manhattan red
Between the adult movie and the
unmade bed 40
Mixed drink is daiquiri green
Between the gospel mission and the sheen
Of hair oil on the rose planted paper.
Mixed drink is forgiveness
Between the vicarious sin 45
And the half-empty bottle of gin.
Mixed drink is remembrance between
unshaded
40-watt bulbs hung from the ceiling,
Between the light a man cannot live by, 50
And the better darkness.
Mixed drink is the sign of contradiction.

The third Bad Sign is this:
"We Serve All Faiths."

We serve all faiths: 55
We the morticians.
Tobias is out, he has had it.
We do not bury the dead.
Not, He died, was buried and after three
days arose. 60
But He died, was revived, and after three
days was buried alive.
This is our scripture.
Do not disturb the established practitioner.
Do not disturb the traditional mortician: 65
Giving fans to the church, for hot days,
Dropping a calendar at the nursing home,
A pamphlet in the hospital waiting room,
An ad in the testimonial brochure at the
retirement banquet. 70
Promising the right music, the artificial grass.
We bury faith of all kinds.
Foreverness does not come easily.
The rates should be higher.

Thomas McGrath

Something Is Dying Here

In a hundred places in North Dakota
Tame locomotives are sleeping
Inside the barricades of bourgeois flowers:
Zinnias, petunias, johnny-jump-ups—
Their once wild fur warming the public squares. 5
Something is dying here.
                And perhaps I, too—
My brain already full of the cloudy lignite of eternity . . .

I invoke an image of my strength.
                Nothing will come. 10
Oh—a homing lion perhaps
                made entirely of tame bees;
Or the chalice of an old storage battery, loaded
With the rancid electricity of the nineteen thirties
Cloud harps iconographic blood 15
Rusting in the burnt church of my flesh . . .

But nothing goes forward:
The locomotive never strays out of the flower corral
The mustang is inventing barbwire the bulls
Have put rings in their noses . . . 20
The dead here
Will leave behind a ring of autobodies,
Weather-eaten bones of cars where the stand-off failed—

Stranger: go tell among the Companions:
These dead weren't put down by Cheyennes or Red 25
                Chinese:
The poison of their own sweet country has brought them
                here.

Rod McKuen

Heroes

Salute the G.I. coming from the green
brandishing the ears and tail
    of his yellow enemy.
Hurry or you'll miss it on T.V.

And on the further bank 5
    the white stud lying in the ditch
the golden bridgework missing
from his gaping bloody mouth.

The media
has canonized the white man. 10
The far left claims the hero
    has a yellow tint.

But all the real heroes
    stay in used-car lots
selling bright red autos 15
with shoulder safety belts
for the freeway war at home.

Rod McKuen

Plan

My cousin Max is being married
        on a quiz show.
He is getting a Westinghouse refrigerator
        a Singer sewing machine
a set of furniture from Sears and Roebuck   5
        an ant farm
    a General Electric toaster
and a girl.

It is not enough.
He expects babies and happiness   10
good times and money
and a government that wars on war.

My cousin Max expects too much.

Rod McKuen

Silence Is Golden

If I had a pistol to hold in my hand
I'd hunt down and silence the Good Humour man,
I'd pour sticky ice cream all over his wound
and stop him forever from playing that tune.

For silence is golden on a soft summer day. 5
It's a pity to let strangers take it away.

If ever I get me a license to kill
I'll war on the jukebox and jackhammer till
the wind and the rain rust up all their parts
and the worms and the woodchucks dissect their hearts. 10

For silence is golden and hard to be found,
and killed far too often by the jackhammer's sound.

Eve Merriam

Block Party

On the corner, right angular, facing the park
The Christian Science church, its granite base
Grimed by the city street, engraven "Purity";
Further down, the Free Synagogue chanting,
Flights of angelic pigeons and the gold-rushed plane to California. 5
Rising prices at the A&P where the women roll their groundmeat
menus home;
Baby carriages, children on skates, laundry handtruck,
Grocer's boy pedaling, police prowl car,
Elephant vans, postman humped with bills and dues, 10
Dogs walking their owners,
Someone moving out, his alter ego in,
So any day wheels on all motion and commotion.

The cigar-store owner with the gray newspaper skin
Shrugs at his unsold pile. 15
"I didn't order so many. The big dealers tell me what I have to
take."
Cashes a relief check, notarizes disaster.
Rings up a deposit of coke.
His wife shrills at the penny youngsters banging the door, 20
Popsicle-dripping over the silkslick magazines,
But her eyes give her away, a tune sweet and true.
She sighs: "May they never grow up to go to war again."

The garbage cans clatter: Keep Your City Clean.
Wrappered housewives undo their mops 25
On the vacant lot next door.
From her crowded vacant window, the penthouse woman.
The Irish elevator runner gabs with the Negro doorman,
Leaves him to eat his lunch alone.

Delivery to the duplex 30
Where the advertising executive, married mistress, and baby mink
daughter

All are analyzing their dreams.
Basement-stooped, the tailor knots his threadbare flesh.
May the heart hold. 35

Some final passion has made the early edition,
And the sign reads anew "Room to let."
No story in the widow dying in the arms of her
Unpaid gas and electric bill.
The sculptor seeks a definitive curve in clay, 40
The writer woos his notebook,
The painter goes elsewhere for material.

The day is sunlight in winter, and the kid sister takes courage,
Steps out of line for a minute, talks back to her older brother:
"You're not the boss of the whole wide world"! 45

Twilight turns on,
The bar-and-grill proclaims neon Hallelujah,
The victor in the televised wrestling bout.
The facsimile French restaurant douses winey sauce
Over the single woman and her lending library nights, 50
Over the older man and his young companion
St. Christopher pendants calming their throbbing Tahitian shirts.

The separate lights go on in all the separate rooms.
Was that someone at the door?
No, it's only the Negro maid. 55
I thought I heard someone at the door.
Only the old man home again from work.
Are you sure there's no one at the door?
Only, murmurs the adolescent, lonely me.

And now it is night, 60
Black-bordering night of the official proclamation
Commanding us each to deeper separateness.
All-out for more unliving.
The State of National Emergency declares
There is an Emperor and he does wear clothes; 65
Windows are not for a view of the street,
But peephole spying.

Oh let us take shelter not out of catastrophe
Playing prone to the make-believe air raid warden,
Huddling back to back under pretended attack from un-sky. 70

What warning, what wedding will unite us
So that a river of light will run leaping through the walls
Unfolding our purse-fisted hands to open palms,
Lifting us higher than the stars, level with one another's eyes,
Seeing ourselves beautifully workday common and Sunday varied, 75
My neighborhood block unbossed, replanned
With doors, windows, and the whole world opening wide?

Eve Merriam

Robin Hood

has returned
to Sherwood Forest
as
Secretary of the Interior

and the greenery 5
is to be preserved
for the public good

directly alongside
the parts reserved
for Hood enterprises 10

for Sherwood Homesites
Shop-and-Sher Parking Plaza
and
Sherburger Franchises.

Eve Merriam

Landscaping

Some of
the more expensive lobbies
now have
mixed in with the artificial
so cunningly 5
you can scarcely tell they are
real plantings

only when
brown spots appear
can you be sure 10
they are real
because then you know they are
dying

Eve Merriam

Tryst

When we were married eight years,
we saved up enough money
for my husband to buy me
an engagement ring.
I wear it to the office 5
to take dictation from the boss,
but then when I go to type
I take it off and
hide it in my cosmetic bag,
you never know with the 10
messengers or temporaries
the agencies send around.
Then when I finish up
at the end of the day,
I go to the ladies' room and 15
hang it on a chain
around my neck,
that way I don't have to
worry in the subway.
Cooking or doing the dishes, 20
I hide it in the candy jar
mixed in with the mints,
nobody would ever look there
and sometimes I find new places
like in the plaid stamp books, 25
it's hard even for me
to know all the nooks where
I put it.
Sometimes I think
when I take off my nightgown 30
for us to make love
I ought to
put it on,
it's really beautiful,
but there's enough 35

to worry about then
on my mind,
I don't want
more responsibility.

Eve Merriam

from Aesop in Washington

5. THE BOY WHO CRIED

There once was a young shepherd tending his flock
all alone. "Help, help!" he cried out, "smog is
polluting the grazing land!"

But nobody listened.

A short time later he cried out, "Help! O please   5
help! Nerve gas has killed the sheep by the
thousands!"

Still nobody listened.

Then he called out, "O look, a black panther
carrying a gun."   10

And everybody came running.

MORAL: Out of God's mouth into public relations

Eve Merriam

Hairy/Scary

youth
grows
like tendrils like curly pubic vines

growing
their sideburns and beards 5
dark as jews

growing
even when theyre sleeping
jesus

creeping 10
choking
clogging

growing
thicker and
crazywild 15

like pedestrians
outrunning cars
it cant be done

but theyre doing it in
growing numbers 20
of course it is hairyscary

and at the head of it
you know who
all those blacks their negrow

afrokinks bulging 25
like a jungle steaming in the midst of
pennsylvania avenue

who will they stew in a pot
got to cut it
got to mow it 30

got to slow it down before it
tell you what
why not

defoliate
the whole 35
unshaven lot

Arthur Miller

Lines from California

They meet for purchase or sale
And to trace their bounds through rosebushes.

There is a catechism: What's your name, what
do you do, how do you feel, and where you from?

Like people on a perpetual cruise, and the dead 5
go overboard into a lawn. It's a deck,
part of which is always on fire.

Anything inconsequential makes them serious.

Some teach parakeets to climb ladders; they also
have Malted Milk Specialists. 10

Tragedy is when you lose your boat.

Life is a preparation for retirement.

The sun is good for business.

Al Jolson left a trust fund which pays
to floodlight his tomb at night forever; 15
even in death a man should have bills.

The second-largest industry is sporting goods.

To succeed as a woman you have to have a car.

California is Christianity plus the conveniences.

Driving from town to town one wonders what will 20
happen if neon gas ever runs out; some may
have to learn to read paint.

When a man admits failure he becomes a pedestrian.

U.S. 30-130
SOUTH
FLYING
FLYING
SERVICE
BAR GRILL
LIQUOR
SUNOCO
EAST
30
BAIRD BLV'D.
DRIVE
WINES
FROM ALL
OVER THE
GREEN
STAMPS

WHITE TOWER

Brotherhood is when two men have the same mother.

Sacrifice is a car sold at a ridiculous price. 25

Society is when people listen to classical music;
or a Savings & Loan.

Law is order, Justice a decent return on money.

Progress is anything turning on and off by itself.

Beauty is teeth, deep skin, and the willingness. 30

Freedom is the right to live among your own kind.

A philosophy is a keen sense of land values
and the patience to wait.

War is peace waged by other means.

They know they are the Future. 35

They are exceedingly well-armed.

Robert Pack

Burning the Laboratory

For months I have been planning it.
The time had come, nothing having changed.
Almost like clockwork, the watchman, shortly
After midnight, begins to doze, his head bobbing
On his shoulders like a swimmer. 5
Occasionally a twitch will wake him, hair
Falling into his eyes—but I must chance that.
About one-thirty, Dr. Wunsch, always last,
Will leave, followed by his hunched back
And unfinished thoughts. He ignores the watchman 10
Who, in his sleep, expects him, dreaming
The truth. I will smack the watchman's head
With a pipe (hopefully not injuring him),
Take his keys and, guided by the floor plan
(Sent to me by the State as a public service), 15
I will, in less than four minutes, achieve
The basement where I will set three time-bombs
I have myself made: one by the heating plant;
One by the electrical control unit;
And one just for good luck. I will leave 20
By the delivery entrance in the back.
If all goes well, the building should not
Collapse, but fires should break out all over,
Though, of course, I cannot know how
The various chemicals and equipment 25
Will react. Perhaps, on the second floor,
The fixed brains of the white rats will jerk open,
Prescribed memories and the tinkered past
Will fall away; perhaps a saving word
Will shape the split, groping lips of the rat leader. 30
It is possible. Like peace.

Marge Piercy

Community

Loving feels lonely in a violent world,
irrelevant to people burning like last year's weeds
with bellies distended, with fish throats agape
and flesh melting down to glue.
We can no longer shut out the screaming 5
that leaks through the ventilation system,
the small bits of bone in the processed bread,
so we are trying to make a community
warm, loose as hair but shaped like a weapon.
Caring, we must use each other to death. 10
Love is arthritic. Mistrust swells like a prune.
Perhaps we gather so they may dig one big cheap grave.
From the roof of the Pentagon which is our Bastille
the generals armed like Martians watch through binoculars
the campfires of draftcards and barricades on the grass. 15
All summer helicopters whine over the ghetto.
Casting up jetsam of charred fingers and torn constitutions
the only world breaks on the door of morning.
We have to build our city, our camp
from used razorblades and bumpers and aspirin boxes 20
in the shadow of the nuclear plant that kills the fish
with coke bottle lamps flickering
on the chemical night.

Marge Piercy

Homo Faber: The Shell Game

Pyramids of flesh sweat pyramids of stone.
Each slave chiseled his cheap as dust life in rock,
with labor dragged from him he marked his own grave
heaped over the painted chrysalis.
The Roman slaves built stadia and roads for empire and trade. 5
Cathedrals: parallel vaulted hands the color of winter clouds
where choirs of polyphonic light strike chilly slabs
while nobles with swords on and skinny saints lie under the
floor.
Fortresses, dungeons, keeps, moats and walls. 10
Skyscrapers where nobody lives filled with paper.
Where do the people live and what have they made themselves
splendid as these towers of glass, these groves of stone?
The impulse that in 1910 molded banks as temples,
where now does it build its central artifact? 15
The ziggurat, the acropolis, the palace of our dream
whose shape rings in the blood's cave like belladonna,
all scream in the eagle's preyseeking swoop of the bomber,
those planes expensive as cities,
the sharklean submarines of death, 20
the taut kinetic tower of the missile,
the dark fiery omphalos of the bomb.

Marge Piercy

I Am a Light You Could Read By

A flame from each finger,
my hands are candelabra,
my hair stands in a torch.
Out of my mouth a long flame hovers.
Can't anyone see, handing me a newspaper? 5
Can't anyone see, stamping my book overdue?
I walk blazing along Sixth Avenue,
burning gas blue I buy subway tokens,
a bouquet of coals, I cross the bridge.
Invisible I singe strangers and pass. 10
Now I am on your street.
How your window flickers.
I come bringing my burning body
like an armful of tigerlilies,
like a votive lantern, 15
like a roomful of tassels and leopards and grapes
for you to come into,
dance in my burning
and we will flare up together like stars
and fall to sleep. 20

Marge Piercy

Learning Experience

The boy sits in the classroom
in Gary, in the United States, in NATO, in SEATO
in the thing-gorged belly of the sociobeast
in fluorescent light in slowly moving time
in boredom thick and greasy as vegetable shortening. 5
The classroom has green boards and ivory blinds,
the desks are new and the teachers not so old.
I have come out on the train from Chicago to talk
about dangling participles. I am supposed
to teach him to think a little on demand. 10
The time of tomorrow's draft exam is written on the board.
The boy yawns and does not want to be in the classroom in
Gary
where the furnaces that consumed his father seethe rusty smoke
and pour cascades of nerve-bright steel 15
while the slag goes out in little dumpcars smoking,
but even less does he want to be in Today's Action Army
in Vietnam, in the Dominican Republic, in Guatemala,
in death that hurts.
In him are lectures on small groups, Jacksonian democracy, 20
French irregular verbs, the names of friends
around him in the classroom in Gary in the pillshaped afternoon
where tomorrow he will try and fail his license to live.

Marge Piercy

Simple-song

When we are going toward someone we say
you are just like me
your thoughts are my brothers
word matches word
how easy to be together. 5

When we are leaving someone we say
how strange you are
we cannot communicate
we can never agree
how hard, hard and weary to be together. 10

We are not different nor alike
but each strange in his leather body
sealed in skin and reaching out clumsy hands
and loving is an act
that cannot outlive 15
the open hand
the open eye
the door in the chest standing open.

Marge Piercy

The Morning Half-life Blues

Girls buck the wind in the grooves toward work
in fuzzy coats promised to be warm as fur.
The shop windows snicker
flashing them hurrying over dresses they cannot afford:
you are not pretty enough, not pretty enough. 5

Blown with yesterday's papers through the boiled coffee morning
they dream of the stop on the subway without a name,
the door in the heart of the grove of skyscrapers,
that garden where we nestle to the teats of a furry world,
lie in mounds of peony eating grapes, 10
and need barter ourselves for nothing,
not by the hour, not by the pound, not by the skinful,
that party to which no one will give or sell them the key
though we have all thought briefly we had found it
drunk or in bed. 15

Black girls with thin legs and high necks stalking like herons,
plump girls with blue legs and green eyelids and strawberry
        breasts,
swept off to be frozen in fluorescent cubes,
the vacuum of your jobs sucks your brains dry 20
and fills you with the ooze of melted comics.
Living is later. This is your rented death.
You grasp at specific commodities and vague lusts
to make up, to pay for each day
which opens like a can and is empty, and then another, 25
afternoons like dinosaur eggs stuffed with glue.

        Girls of the dirty morning, ticketed and spent,
you will be less at forty than at twenty.
Your living is a waste product of somebody's mill.
I would fix you like buds to a city where people work 30
to make and do things necessary and good,
where work is real as bread and babies and trees in parks
and you would blossom slowly and ripen to sound fruit.

Marge Piercy

To Grow On

The first chickyellow probes of sun
fluffy with mopdust
touch the windows.
Nothing here is quite
smooth or whole. 5
The pipes weep rust,
boards sag and heave,
plaster sighs into dust
and from the ceiling tatter
winsome stalactites 10
of paint.

On the ledges
old paint blisters into maps.
Chips of pretty paint
snow on the crib. 15
Paint, the landlord's friend,
holds up the walls.
All winter children peck it.

In the first cornsyrup pools of sun
small fingers uncoil 20
like germinating beans.
Fingers: test tubes
for that simple chemistry:
sun activates the lead
winter's swallowed drifts 25
whose tired colors now
run through the blood.

Death blooms with the
suburban hyacinths.
Even spring 30
charges a little more
to the poor.

Marge Piercy

Why the Soup Tastes like the Daily News

The great dream stinks like a whale gone aground.
Somewhere in New York Harbor
in the lee of the iron maiden
it died of pollution
and was cast up on Cape Cod by the Provincetown Light. 5
The vast blubber is rotting.
Scales of fat ripple on the waters
until the taste of that decay
like a sulphurous factory of chemical plenty
dyes every tongue. 10

Sylvia Plath

The Thin People

They are always with us, the thin people
Meager of dimension as the grey people

On a movie-screen. They
Are unreal, we say:

It was only in a movie, it was only 5
In a war making evil headlines when we

Were small that they famished and
Grew so lean and would not round

Out their stalky limbs again though
peace 10
Plumped the bellies of the mice

Under the meanest table.
It was during the long hunger-battle

They found their talent to persevere
In thinness, to come, later, 15

Into our bad dreams, their menace
Not guns, not abuses,

But a thin silence.
Wrapped in flea-ridden donkey skins.

Empty of complaint, forever 20
Drinking vinegar from tin cups: they
wore

The insufferable nimbus of the lot-drawn
Scapegoat. But so thin,

So weedy a race could not remain in 25
dreams,
Could not remain outlandish victims

In the contracted country of the head
Any more than the old woman in her
mud hut could 30

Keep from cutting fat meat
Out of the side of the generous moon
  when it

Set foot nightly in her yard
Until her knife had pared 35

The moon to a rind of little light.
Now the thin people do not obliterate

Themselves as the dawn
Greyness blues, reddens, and the outline

Of the world comes clear and fills with 40
  color.
They persist in the sunlit room: the wall-
  paper

Frieze of cabbage-roses and cornflowers
  pales 45
Under their thin-lipped smiles,

Their withering kingship.
How they prop each other up!

We own no wildernesses rich and deep
  enough 50
For stronghold against their stiff

Battalions. See, how the tree boles flatten
And lose their good browns

If the thin people simply stand in the
  forest, 55
Making the world go thin as a wasp's
  nest

And greyer; not even moving their bones.

Sylvia Plath

Mushrooms

Overnight, very
Whitely, discreetly,
Very quietly

Our toes, our noses
Take hold on the loam, 5
Acquire the air.

Nobody sees us,
Stops us, betrays us;
The small grains make room.

Soft fists insist on 10
Heaving the needles,
The leafy bedding,

Even the paving.
Our hammers, our rams,
Earless and eyeless, 15

Perfectly voiceless,
Widen the crannies,
Shoulder through holes. We

Diet on water,
On crumbs of shadow, 20
Bland-mannered, asking

Little or nothing.
So many of us!
So many of us!

We are shelves, we are 25
Tables, we are meek,
We are edible,

Nudgers and shovers
In spite of ourselves.
Our kind multiplies:

We shall by morning
Inherit the earth.
Our foot's in the door.

Alastair Reid

Curiosity

may have killed the cat; more likely
the cat was just unlucky, or else curious
to see what death was like, having no cause
to go on licking paws, or fathering
litter on litter of kittens, predictably. 5

Nevertheless, to be curious
is dangerous enough. To distrust
what is always said, what seems,
to ask odd questions, interfere in dreams,
leave home, smell rats, have hunches 10
does not endear him to those doggy circles
where well-smelt baskets, suitable wives, good lunches
are the order of things, and where prevails
much wagging of incurious heads and tails.

Face it. Curiosity 15
will not cause him to die—
only lack of it will.
Never to want to see
the other side of the hill,
or that improbable country 20
where living is an idyll
(although a probable hell)
would kill us all.
Only the curious
have, if they live, a tale 25
worth telling at all.

Dogs say he loves too much, is irresponsible,
is changeable, marries too many wives,
deserts his children, chills all dinner tables
with tales of his nine lives. 30
Well, he is lucky. Let him be
nine-lived and contradictory,
curious enough to change, prepared to pay

the cat price, which is to die
and die again and again, 35
each time with no less pain.
A cat minority of one
is all that can be counted on
to tell the truth. And what he has to tell
on each return from hell 40
is this: that dying is what the living do,
and dying is what the loving do,
and that dead dogs are those who do not know
that hell is where, to live, they have to go.

Kenneth Rexroth

A Sword in a Cloud of Light

Your hand in mine, we walk out
To watch the Christmas Eve crowds
On Fillmore Street, the Negro
District. The night is thick with
Frost. The people hurry, wreathed 5
In their smoky breaths. Before
The shop windows the children
Jump up and down with spangled
Eyes. Santa Clauses ring bells.
Cars stall and honk. Streetcars clang. 10
Loudspeakers on the lampposts
Sing carols, on jukeboxes
In the bars Louis Armstrong
Plays *White Christmas.* In the joints
The girls strip and grind and bump 15
To *Jingle Bells.* Overhead
The neon signs scribble and
Erase and scribble again
Messages of avarice,
Joy, fear, hygiene, and the proud 20
Names of the middle classes.
The moon beams like a pudding.
We stop at the main corner
And look up diagonally
Across, at the rising moon, 25
And the solemn, orderly
Vast winter constellations.
You say, "There's Orion!"
The most beautiful object
Either of us will ever 30
Know in the world or in life
Stands in the moonlit empty
Heavens, over the swarming
Men, women and children, black
And white, joyous and greedy, 35
Evil and good, buyer and

Seller, master and victim,
Like some immense theorem,
Which, if once solved would forever
Solve the mystery and pain 40
Under the bells and spangles.
There he is, the man of the
Night before Christmas, spread out
On the sky like a true god
In whom it would only be 45
Necessary to believe
A little. I am fifty
And you are five. It would do
No good to say this and it
May do no good to write it. 50
Believe in Orion. Believe
In the night, the moon, the crowded
Earth. Believe in Christmas and
Birthdays and Easter rabbits.
Believe in all those fugitive 55
Compounds of nature, all doomed
To waste away and go out.
Always be true to these things.
They are all there is. Never
Give up this savage religion 60
For the blood drenched civilized
Abstractions of the rascals
Who live by killing you and me.

Theodore Roethke

Dolor

I have known the inexorable sadness of pencils,
Neat in their boxes, dolor of pad and paper-weight,
All the misery of manilla folders and mucilage,
Desolation in immaculate public places,
Lonely reception room, lavatory, switchboard, 5
The unalterable pathos of basin and pitcher,
Ritual of multigraph, paper-clip, comma,
Endless duplication of lives and objects.
And I have seen dust from the walls of institutions,
Finer than flour, alive, more dangerous than silica, 10
Sift, almost invisible, through long afternoons of tedium,
Dropping a fine film on nails and delicate eyebrows,
Glazing the pale hair, the duplicate gray standard faces.

Stephen Sandy

The Woolworth Philodendron

Among the plastic flowers one honest one
Graced Woolworth's floor: a real dodo in a green-
house of smilax and excelsior, a sort of proto-
Gew-gaw, if you please, it was so dada
In that museum of small cheers, 5
Leaves snapped and torn by the sheer
Relentless legs of ladies foraging
For comfort; in a plastic pot, the real thing.

Suspecting it alive, I brought it home.
Five months it sulked in a leafless dream; 10
Through grillings by the daily sun it never broke
Its dimestore trance, tight-lipped as rock.
And now it is April in the pliant bones and strange
To note the beaten juices fuse and plunge:
A green prong spirals up to the blaze, unplugs 15
Revenge for ladies' grazing and ungrateful legs.

The shoppers' world is washed away—how fine
To see my green tooth cut the sunshine
And make a brittle pact with the sun's plan!
But it's more than the tender gesture of a jungle vine. 20
I watch it coil to careful multiplicity
Through my weeks of boring work; I have begun to see
A careless wildness, long-leaved and green,
Mesh with dark plots implicit in the sun.

Delmore Schwartz

The True-Blue American

Jeremiah Dickson was a true-blue American,
For he was a little boy who understood America, for he
felt that he must
Think about *everything;* because that's all there is to
think about, 5
Knowing immediately the intimacy of truth and comedy,
Knowing intuitively how a sense of humor was a necessity
For one and for all who live in America. Thus, natively,
and
Naturally when on an April Sunday in an ice cream 10
parlor Jeremiah
Was requested to choose between a chocolate sundae
and a banana split
He answered unhesitatingly, having no need to think of it
Being a true-blue American, determined to continue as 15
he began:
Rejecting the either-or of Kierkegaard, and many another
European;
Refusing to accept alternatives, refusing to believe the
choice of between; 20
Rejecting selection; denying dilemma; electing absolute
affirmation: knowing
in his breast
The infinite and the gold
Of the endless frontier, the deathless West. 25

"Both: I will have them both!" declared this true-blue
American
In Cambridge, Massachusetts, on an April Sunday, instructed
By the great department stores, by the Five-and-Ten,
Taught by Christmas, by the circus, by the vulgarity and 30
grandeur of
Niagara Falls and the Grand Canyon,
Tutored by the grandeur, vulgarity, and infinite appetite
gratified and
Shining in the darkness, of the light 35

On Saturdays at the double bills of the moon pictures,
The consummation of the advertisements of the imagination
of the light
Which is as it was— the infinite belief in infinite hope—
of Columbus 40
Barnum, Edison, and Jeremiah Dickson.

F. R. Scott

Examiner

The routine trickery of the examination
Baffles these hot and discouraged youths.
Driven by they know not what external pressure
They pour their hated self-analysis
Through the nib of confession, onto the accusatory page. 5

I, who have plotted their immediate downfall,
I am entrusted with the divine categories,
ABCD and the hell of E,
The parade of prize and the backdoor of pass.

In the tight silence 10
Standing by the green grass window
Watching the fertile earth graduate its sons
With more compassion—not commanding the shape
Of stem and stamen, bringing the trees to pass
By shift of sunlight and increase of rain, 15
For each seed the whole soil, for the inner life
The environment receptive and contributory—
I shudder at the narrow frames of our text-book schools
In which we plant our so various seedlings.
Each brick-walled barracks 20
Cut into numbered rooms, black-boarded,
Ties the venturing shoot to the master stick;
The screw-desk rows of lads and girls
Subdued in the shade of an adult—
Their acid subsoil— 25
Shape the new to the old in the ashen garden.
Shall we open the whole skylight of thought
To these tiptoe minds, bring them our frontier worlds
And the boundless uplands of art for their field of
growth? 30

Or shall we pass them the chosen poems with the foot-
notes,
Ring the bell on their thoughts, period their play,

Make laws for averages and plans for means,
Print one history for a whole province, and 35
Let ninety thousand reach page 10 by Tuesday?

As I gather the inadequate paper evidence, I hear
Across the neat campus lawn
The professional mowers drone, clipping the inch-high
green. 40

Harvey Shapiro

In Our Day

Society
Turning its past
To glorious junk,
Like the artist,
In our day. 5
Free-floating
Liberation
As a style
In the street.
Everybody 10
Playing
In the muck
Of the imagination,
Finger-painting
The walls 15
For psychic health.
The mind's rigor
Become
A sunlit field.

Harvey Shapiro

National Cold Storage Company

The National Cold Storage Company contains
More things than you can dream of.
Hard by the Brooklyn Bridge it stands
In a litter of freight cars,
Tugs to one side; the other, the traffic 5
Of the Long Island Expressway.
I myself have dropped into it in seven years
Midnight tossings, plans for escape, the shakes.
Add this to the national total–
Grant's tomb, the Civil War, Arlington, 10
The young President dead.
Above the warehouse and beneath the stars
The poets creep on the harp of the Bridge.
But see,
They fall into the National Cold Storage Company 15
One by one. The wind off the river is too cold,
Or the times too rough, or the Bridge
Is not a harp at all. Or maybe
A monstrous birth inside the warehouse
Must be fed by everything–ships, poems, 20
Stars, all the years of our lives.

Karl Shapiro

The Conscientious Objector

The gate clanged and they walked you into jail
More tense than felons but relieved to find
The hostile world shut out, the flags that dripped
From every mother's windowpane, obscene
The bloodlust sweating from the public heart, 5
The dog authority slavering at your throat.
A sense of quiet, of pulling down the blind
Possessed you. Punishment you felt was clean.

The decks, the catwalks, and the narrow light
Composed a ship. This was a mutinous crew 10
Troubling the captains for plain decencies,
A *Mayflower* brim with pilgrims headed out
to establish new theocracies to west,
A Noah's ark coasting the topmost seas
Ten miles above the sodomites and fish. 15
These inmates loved the only living doves.

Like all men hunted from the world you made
A good community, voyaging the storm
To no safe Plymouth or green Ararat;
Trouble or calm, the men with Bibles prayed, 20
The gaunt politicals construed our hate.
The opposite of all armies, you were best
Opposing uniformity and yourselves;
Prison and personality were your fate.

You suffered not so physically but knew 25
Maltreatment, hunger, ennui of the mind.
Well might the soldier kissing the hot beach
Erupting in his face damn all your kind.
Yet you who saved neither yourselves nor us
Are equally with those who shed the blood 30
The heroes of our cause. Your conscience is
What we come back to in the armistice.

Paul Simon

Dangling Conversation

It's a still life water color,
Of a now late afternoon,
As the sun shines through the curtain lace,
And shadows wash the room.

And we sit and drink our coffee, 5
Couched in our indifference,
Like shells upon the shore.
You can hear the ocean roar,
In the dangling conversation
And the superficial sighs, 10
The borders of our lives.

And you read your Emily Dickinson,
And I my Robert Frost,
And we note our place with bookmarkers
That measure what we've lost. 15

Like a poem poorly written,
We are verses out of rhythm,
Couplets out of rhyme,
In syncopated time,
And the dangling conversation
And the superficial sighs, 20
Are the borders of our lives.

Yes we speak of things that matter,
With words that must be said,
Can analysis be worthwhile,
Is the theatre really dead? 25

Now the room is softly faded,
And I only kiss your shadow,
I cannot feel your hand,
You're a stranger now unto me,
Lost in the dangling conversation, 30
And the superficial sighs,
In the borders of our lives.

Paul Simon

The Sound of Silence

Hello darkness my old friend,
I've come to talk with you again,
Because a vision softly creeping,
Left its seeds while I was sleeping,
And the vision that was planted in my brain 5
Still remains within the sound of silence.

In restless dreams I walked alone
Narrow streets of cobble-stone,
'Neath the halo of a street lamp,
I turned my collar to the cold and damp
When my eyes were stabbed by the flash of a neon light
That split the night and touched the sound of silence.

And in the naked light I saw
Ten thousand people maybe more.
People talking without speaking, 15
People hearing without listening,
People writing songs that voices never share
And no one dare disturb the sound of silence.

"Fools!" said I, "You do not know
Silence like a cancer grows. 20
Hear my words that I might teach you,
Take my arms that I might reach you."
But my words like silent raindrops fell,
And echoed in the wells of silence.

And the people bowed and prayed 25
To the neon god they made.
And the sign flashed out its warning.
In the words that it was forming,
And the sign said:
"The words of the prophets are written 30
on the subway walls and tenement halls"
And whispered in the sounds of silence.

L. E. Sissman

from A War Requiem

23. CAMBRIDGE, 1963

A wake, without the whiskey or the words
Of eulogy, before the one blue eye
Of television in the deepening
November evening. When, earlier,
My secretary said she'd heard that he 5
Had just been shot, we gaped in nervous pre-
Lapsarian unbelief. Not it is not
More real but we are less so, and the screen
Calls us to places in a doomsday scene
Of national disjuncture from a show 10
By Wells or Welles. Lear's "never," a hoarse crow
Of omen, takes wing to the rooky wood
Of early terrors suddenly grown up,
Grown old in one weekend. A catafalque
On wagon wheels rolls, powered by muffled drums, 15
Down the vast desert street to which we come,
Clutching our wives and wallets, to assist
In turning nature art; in the night mist
Behind the White House, two linked silhouettes—
A great *Life* picture—cut across the lawn 20
To leave the sound stage and to be alone.

25. TALKING UNION, 1964

The liberator of the laboring
Classes is interviewed on "Meet the Press."
The ruffian who led the Frontenac
Sitdown is missing; his aged surrogate 25
Is a stout statesman, silver-polled and -tongued,
And silver-tied over a white-on-white
Dress shirt under a trig, if Portly, suit
Tailored by Weatherill. His priestly, bluff
Face with its large pores dryly swallows up 30
All pointed questions; his brown coin-purse mouth
Doles out small change wrapped in the florid scrip
Of Federalese: "parameters," "key gains,"

"judgmentally," "negated," "targeting,"
"So, gentlemen; you see." So gentlemen 35
Are made, not born, with infinite labor pains.

28. NEW YORK, 1967

Eyes flick blades out from under low lids, and
Turn down again to fasten on the sparks
Struck by the sidewalk. My eyes meet that tide
Halfway: the same aloofness, the same stab 40
Of quick cognition, the same lowering
Of sights to shoe lane, having sized them up
And put them down for good. The girls require
A little longer for each dancing breast
And mincing leg. Only the mannequins 45
In Bonwit's windows render me a straight,
Bland stare, which I return in kind. The Pan
Am Building, in its jointed corridors,
Affords relief: acquaintances are cut
Off neatly by their bends, and nearer friends 50
Truncated, disembodied, guillotined
By abstract passages and unseen doors
In a new social contract of surreal
Withdrawal and avoidance, an absurd
Theatre without end and without word. 55

29. TWO CANDIDATES, 1968

A private conversation in a room
Rife with the public and the press. Amid
White sheets of flashlight, the hot, desperate
Advance men poised to seize the candidate
And whisk him to his next engagement, late 60
As ever, he lets fall a casual
Comment upon the state of poetry;
Laughs lightly over an egregious lie
Expounded by an arch-opponent; cites
The over-erudite allusions of 65
Another rival to the ancient Greek.
"That's Aeschylation in political
Quotation," he remarks in a slow, calm
Voice at the middle of the maelstrom.

The other office seeker occupies 70
A lidded bed under the gritty eyes
Of gleaming notabilities, a guard
Of honor changed at each night hour; the eyes

Of those unknowns who, in a double line,
Reach backward, out the great church doors, around 75
The block behind the buttresses; the eyes
Of early watchers high up in the sun-
Struck monolith across the street, who see,
At length, a coffin carried out; the eyes
Of mourners at the stops along a route 80
Just the reverse of Lincoln's; the dry eyes
Of the most high and lowly in the long,
Decayed, redounding concourse of the Un-
Ion Station; late, the eyes of Washington.

30. NEW YORK, 1968

The surf of traffic in the arteries 85
Of evening inundates all ears; in crosstown streets,
It is occluded by occasional
Yells, ashcans falling, Sanitation trucks
Regurgitating garbage, witching cries,
A crystalline lone footstep with a limp, 90
And Robinson's phone ringing in his flat.
Still, sometimes our small noise and voice are heard
Above the melancholy, long, advancing roar
Of transit reaching up the beach of our
Old ananthropocentric island, to 95
The bass of the night wind, and we come true
To one another, till the rising town's
Unhuman voices wake us, and we drown.

31. THIRTY THOUSAND GONE, 1968

In CONUS, whence all blessings flow, I drive
To Ayer for beer. On the road, amber flares 100
Ripen like grapefruit in a grove of air
Fast growing dark. Down in the valley, small-
Calibre guns begin long, gibbering
Dialogues out beyond the mock Perfume
River, really the smelly Nashua. 105
Tank engines ululate. In Vietnam
Village, street fighters infiltrate the set
Of simulated buildings, while flechette
Canisters fired by 105s protect
The point with sheets of tissue-shredding darts. 110
The heavies enter. Flashes shatter night
And Impacts puncture my unruffled drum
Roll of exhaust. In Ayer, the archetype
Of post towns, with its scruffy yellow-brick

Two-story business blocks, shut shops, bright bars, 115
It's pay night. In the orchid neon light
Shed by the Little Klub, a herd of ponycars
Grazes an asphalt pasture. Feat M.P.s
Snuff out a flash fight at the Hotel Linc.
A Charger burns a little rubber to 120
Arrest two ready, wary, cruising girls
Whose buttocks counter-rotate down Main Street.
'Nam veterans in troop boots and a chest
Awash with medal ribbons stare down knots
Of new recruits, high on Colt 45. 125
The Package Store is all decorum. Men
In black bow ties wait coolly on the boys,
Their guns and clubs prudentially concealed
Behind the counter. With my six-pack, I
Leave town, passing an Army ambulance 130
With beacon on and siren winnowing
The road ahead. A yellow GTO
Has flipped atop the railroad bridge, and bare-
Armed viewers with mauve cheeks, purpureal
Eyes, lavender-green lips in mercury- 135
Vapor-lamp light look on in ecstasy
At others' errors. From the overpass
On the road back, I see a divisional
Convoy bound westward, double strands of lights
Strung clear back to the third ridge, coming on 140
Slowly, preserving prescribed intervals,
Diminishing the other way in one
Long red ellipsis, going, going, gone
Into the red crack that still separates
The blue-black air from blue-black earth: the gates 145
At the world's end. The battle on our hill
Still rants and tatters nighttime till a red
Flare, like a larger Mars, can supervene
And make a false arrest of everything.
The last burst dies; the battlefield goes dark; 150
Cicadas sizzle; towns away, dogs bark.

L. E. Sissman

from A Day in the City

IV. EAST FORTY-SECOND STREET

Acutely, the late sun interrogates
The street held in its custody, casting
New light on western faces, shadowing
Each subject with the long arm of the law
Of relativity, gilding the back, 5
Benighting the east front of everyone.
In front of Longchamps, on a burning brass
Standpipe stained orange by sundown, a tall green
Girl worth her weight in meadows, orchards, trees
Sits waiting for her date to claim her long 10
Cool fall champaign, capped by black scuds of curls,
And stage a pastoral with her as Phyllis
And him as Colin, awkward, forward, witty,
Against the pre-cast forest of the city.

L. E. Sissman

Sweeney to Mrs. Porter in the Spring

In Prospect Street, outside the Splendid Bar
And Grill, the Pepsi generation—
The beardless, hard-eyed future of our nation—
Rolls casually south out of the slum
From which it will go far, 5
Leaving an old country where spring has come.

It is not obvious about the spring.
You have to know the signs: a hoist of wash
On every back-piazza line, a sash
Propped open with an empty pint of cream, 10
A comic softening
Of the wind's blade to rubber, an old dream

Of something better coming soon for each
Survivor who achieves the shores of May—
Perhaps a legacy, a lucky play 15
At dogs or numbers, or a contest prize.
Lady Luck, on the beach
Between assignments, does not hear their cries,

"Me! Me!" like gulls'. She never will. The old
Diminish steadily in all but years 20
And hope, which, uncontrollable as tears,
Racks them with life. Just look at Mrs. Porter,
Preparing to unfold,
In the dark bar, a letter from her daughter,

A beauty operator in Ladue, 25
And to remasticate the lovely tale
Of ranch and Pontiac, washed down with ale
Cold from the Splendid bowels, while waiting for
Her unrefined but true
Love's shape to shade the frosted-glass front door. 30

Meanwhile, Sweeney, Medallion 83
(A low old-timer's number), wheels his hack,

In Independent livery, past a back-
Projected process shot of Central Square,
To where his love will be, 35
Impatient to resume their grand affair.

She, like a pile of black rugs, stirs to hear
His two-tone horn just outside, heralding
The coming of both Sweeney and the spring.
Inside, he greets her as before, "Hi, Keed," 40
While Wilma lays his beer
And whiskey down between them and gets paid.

His knotty fingers, tipped with moons of dirt,
Lock on the shot of Seagram's, which he belts
And chases with a swig of Knick. Nobody else 45
Could comfort them except their old selves, who
Preserve, worn but unhurt,
The common knowledge of a thing or two

They did together under other moons.
Now the Splendid night begins again, 50
Unkinking cares, alleviating pain,
Permitting living memories to flood
This country for old men
With spring, their green tongues speaking from the mud.

W. D. Snodgrass

The Men's Room in the College Chapel

Here, in the most Unchristian basement
of this "fortress for the Christian mind,"
they close these four gray walls, shut out shame,
and scribble of sex and excrement,
draw bestial pictures and sign their name— 5
the old, lewd defiance of mankind.

The subversive human in his cell—
burn his vile books, stamp out his credo,
lock him away where no light falls,
and no live word can go back to tell 10
where he's entombed like Monte Cristo—
still, he'll carve his platform in the walls.

In need, men have painted the deep caves
to summon their animal, dark gods;
even the reviled, early Christians 15
prayed in catacombs to outlawed Good,
laid their honored dead and carved out graves
with pious mottos of resistance.

This is the last cave, where the soul
turns in its corner like a beast 20
nursing its wounds, where it contemplates
vengeance, how it shall gather to full
strength, what lost cause shall it vindicate,
returning, masterless and twisted.

Gary Snyder

A Heifer Clambers Up

a heifer clambers up
    nighthawk goes out
        horses
trail back to the barn.
    spider gleams in his   5
        new web
dew on the shingles, on the car,
    on the mailbox—
the mole, the onion, and the beetle
    cease their wars.   10
      worlds tip
into the sunshine, men and women
    get up, babies crying
children grab their lunches
      and leave for school.   15
the radio announces
    in the milking barn
      in the car bound for work
"tonight all the countries
    will get drunk and have a party"   20

russia, america, china,
        singing with their poets,
pregnant and gracious,
    sending flowers and dancing bears
        to all the capitals   25
fat
    with the baby happy land

Gary Snyder

Above Pate Valley

We finished clearing the last
Section of trail by noon,
High on the ridge-side
Two thousand feet above the creek—
Reached the pass, went on 5
Beyond the white pine groves,
Granite shoulders, to a small
Green meadow watered by the snow,
Edged with Aspen— sun
Straight high and blazing 10
But the air was cool.
Ate a cold fried trout in the
Trembling shadows. I spied
A glitter, and found a flake
Black volcanic glass— obsidian— 15
By a flower. Hands and knees
Pushing the Bear grass, thousands
Of arrowhead leavings over a
Hundred yards. Not one good
Head, just razor flakes 20
On a hill snowed all but summer,
A land of fat summer deer,
They came to camp. On their
Own trails. I followed my own
Trail here. Picked up the cold-drill, 25
Pick, singlejack, and sack
Of dynamite.
Ten Thousand Years.

Gary Snyder

Dawn

Rolling snow turned peach-color
            the moon
   left alone in the fading night
makes a soft cry in the heavens
and once more
drinks up the scattered light

Gary Snyder

Marin-An

sun breaks over the eucalyptus
grove below the wet pasture,
water's about hot,
I sit in the open window
& roll a smoke. 5

distant dogs bark, a pair of
cawing crows; the twang
of a pygmy nuthatch high in a pine—
from behind the cypress windrow
the mare moves up, grazing. 10

a soft continuous roar
comes out of the far valley
of the six-lane highway— thousands
and thousands of cars
driving men to work. 15

Gary Snyder

Mid-August at Sourdough Mountain Lookout

Down valley a smoke haze
Three days heat, after five days rain
Pitch glows in the fir-cones
Across rocks and meadows
Swarms of new flies. 5

I cannot remember things I once read
A few friends, but they are in cities.
Drinking cold snow-water from a tin cup
Looking down for miles
Through high still air. 10

Gary Snyder

This Tokyo

Peace, war, religion,
Revolution, will not help.
This horror seeds in the agile
Thumb and greedy little brain
That learned to catch bananas 5
With a stick.
    The millions of us worthless
To each other or the world
Or selves, the sufferers of the real
Or of the mind—this world 10
Is but a dream? Or human life
A nightmare grafted on solidity
Of planet—mental, mental,
Shudder of the sun—praise
Evil submind freedom with De Sade 15
Or highest Dantean radiance of the God
Or endless Light or Life or Love
Or simple tinsel angel in the
Candy heaven of the poor—
Mental divinity or beauty, all, 20
Plato, Aquinas, Buddha,
Dionysius of the Cross, all
Pains or pleasures hells or
What in sense or flesh
Logic, eye, music, or 25
Concoction of all faculties
& thought tend—tend—to this:
    This gaudy apartment of the rich.
The comfort of the U.S. For its own.
The shy shivering part of girls 30
Who dyked each other for a show
A thousand yen before us men
—In an icy room—to buy their relatives
A meal. This scramble spawn of
Wire dirt rails tin boards blocks 35

Babies, students, crookt old men.
    We live
On the meeting of sun and earth.
We live—we live—and all our lives
Have led to this, this city, 40
Which is soon the world, this
Hopelessness where love of man
Or hate of man could matter
None, love if you will or
Contemplate or write or teach 45
But know in your human marrow you
Who read, that all you tread
Is earthquake rot and matter mental
Trembling, freedom is a void,
Peace war religion revolution 50
Will not help.

William Stafford

Passing Remark

In scenery I like flat country.
In life I don't like much to happen.

In personalities I like mild colorless people.
And in colors I prefer gray and brown.

My wife, a vivid girl from the mountains,
says, "Then why did you choose me?"

Mildly I lower my brown eyes—
there are so many things admirable people
do not understand.

William Stafford

from "The Move to California"

3. AT THE SUMMIT

Past the middle of the continent—
wheatfields turning in God's hand
green to pale to yellow,
like the season gradual—
we approached the summit 5
prepared to face the imminent
map of all our vision,
the sudden look at new land.

As we stopped there, neutral,
standing on the Great Divide, 10
alpine flora, lodgepole pine
fluttering down on either side—
a little tree just three feet high
shared our space between the clouds,
opposing all the veering winds. 15
Unharried, we went down.

4. SPRINGS NEAR HAGERMAN

Water leaps from lava near Hagerman,
piles down riverward over rock
reverberating tons of exploding shock
    out of that stilled world. 20

We halted there once. In that cool
We drank, for back and where we had to go
lay our jobs and Idaho,
    lying far from such water.

At work when I vision that sacred land— 25
the vacation of mist over its rock wall—
I go blind with hope. That plumed fall
    is bright to remember.

5. ALONG HIGHWAY 40

Those who wear green glasses through Nevada
travel a ghastly road in unbelievable cars 30
and lose pale dollars
under violet hoods when they park at gambling houses.

I saw those martyrs—all sure of their cars in the open
and always believers in any handle they pulled—
wracked on an invisible cross
and staring at a green table. 35

While the stars were watching
I crossed the Sierras in my old Dodge
letting the speedometer measure God's kindness,
and slept in the wilderness on the hard ground. 40

6. WRITTEN ON THE STUB OF THE FIRST PAYCHECK

Gasoline makes game scarce.
In Elko, Nevada, I remember a stuffed wildcat
someone had shot on Bing Crosby's ranch.
I stood in the filling station
breathing fumes and reading the snarl of a map. 45

There were peaks to the left so high
they almost got away in the heat;
Reno and Las Vegas were ahead.
I had promise of the California job,
and three kids with me. 50

It takes a lot of miles to equal one wildcat
today. We moved into a housing tract.
Every dodging animal carries my hope in Nevada.
It has been a long day, Bing.
Wherever I go is your ranch. 55

George Starbuck

Of Late

"Stephen Smith, University of Iowa sophomore, burned
                what he said was his draft card"
and Norman Morrison, Quaker, of Baltimore Maryland,
                burned what he said was himself.
You Robert McNamara, burned what you said was a   5
        concentration of the Enemy Aggressor.
No news medium troubled to put it in quotes.

And Norman Morrison, Quaker, of Baltimore Maryland,
                burned what he said was himself.
He said it with simple materials such as would be found   10
                in your kitchen.
In your office you were informed.
Reporters got cracking frantically on the mental disturbance
                angle.
So far nothing turns up.   15

Norman Morrison, Quaker, of Baltimore Maryland, burned
                and while burning, screamed.
No tip-off. No release.
Nothing to quote, to manage to put in quotes.
Pity the unaccustomed hesitance of the newspaper editorialists.   20
Pity the press photographers, not called.

Norman Morrison, Quaker, of Baltimore Maryland, burned
                and was burned and said
all that there is to say in that language.
Twice what is said in yours.   25
It is a strange sect, Mr. McNamara, under advice to try
the whole of a thought in silence, and to oneself.

George Starbuck

from Poems from a First Year in Boston

II. OUTBREAK OF SPRING

Stirring porchpots up with green-fingered witchcraft,
insinuating cats in proper outskirts,
hag Spring in a wink blacks the prim white magic
of winter-wimpled Boston's every matesick
splinter of spinster landscape. 5

Under the matchstick
march of her bridgework, melting, old lady Mystic
twitches her sequins coyly, but the calls
of her small tugs entice no geese. Canals
take freight; the roads throw up stiff hands, and the 10
Charles
arches. Spring's on us: a life raft wakes the waters
of Walden like a butt-slap.

And yet she loiters.
Where is song while the lark in winter quarters 15
lolls? What's to solace Scollay's hashhouse floaters
and sing them to their dolls? and yet—
strange musics,
migrant melodies of exotic ozarks,
twitter and throb where the bubble-throated jukebox 20
lurks iridescent by these lurid newsracks.
Browser leafing here, withhold your wisecracks:
tonight, in public, straight from overseas,
her garish chiaroscuro turned to please
you and her other newsstand devotees, 25
the quarter-lit Diana takes her ease.

So watch your pockets, cats, hang onto your hearts,
for when you've drunk her glitter till it hurts—
Curtain.

Winds frisk you to the bone. 30

Full feasted
Spring, like an ill bird, settles to the masthead,
of here and there an elm. The streets are misted.
A Boston rain, archaic and monastic,
cobbles the blacktop waters, brings mosaic 35
to dusty windshields; to the waking, music.

Dennis Trudell

Going to Pittsburgh

In and between the cities
the go-go girls are bluffing.
They really will not step down
and lie on a corner table.

The men prefer the ones 5
who look most like coeds.
The men have come there
from factories or softball.

Their eyes do not love
one another's eyes; their 10
wives or girlfriends are home
changing sheets or channels.

Their in-laws fail to
understand them, their sons
wear faggoty hair—Something 15
is hungry; it is not fed.

In and between the cities
the night is ungenerous.
The pizza and hamburgers
are thin; hitchhikers freeze. 20

The car-hops don't jounce.
The motels are unfriendly,
their flies bite. Their walls
are sick of self-abortions.

Something is hungry; it is 25
not fed—In the soft suburbs
the martinis aren't working.
The heads of industry are sad.

Their candidates don't win.
Their alma maters won't let 30

them re-enroll; their suicide
notes have comma splices.

In and between the cities
the stares of the blacks
are causing cigarette burns 35
in beds of the middle class.

The husbands do not know
how to load the small arms
they have bought for summer.
They think often of Sweden. 40

They think that in rooms
behind drapes in Negro bars
the Navajos learn karate.
They fear for their stereos.

Something in and between 45
the cities is hungry; it is
not fed. This is no season
to learn the names of birds—

It is no time for that.

David Wagoner

The Man from the Top of the Mind

From immaculate construction to half death,
See him: the light bulb screwed into his head,
The vacuum tube of his sex, the electric eye.
What lifts his foot? What does he do for breath?

His nickel steel, oily from neck to wrist, 5
Glistens as though by sunlight where he stands.
Nerves bought by the inch and muscles on a wheel
Spring in the triple-jointed hooks of his hands.

As plug to socket, or flange upon a beam,
Two become one; yet what is he to us? 10
We cry, "Come, marry the bottom of our minds.
Grant us the strength of your impervium."

But clad in a seamless skin, he turns aside
To do the tricks ordained by his transistors—
His face impassive, his arms raised from the dead, 15
His switch thrown one way into animus.

Reach for him now, and he will flicker with light,
Divide preposterous numbers by unknowns,
Bump through our mazes like a genius rat,
Or trace his concentric echoes to the moon. 20

Then, though we beg him, "Love us, hold us fast,"
He will stalk out of focus in the air,
Make gestures in an elemental mist,
And falter there—as we will falter here

And turns in rage upon our horrible shapes— 25
When the automaton pretends to dream
Those nightmares, trailing shreds of his netherworld,
Who must be slaughtered backward into time.

Chad Walsh

Port Authority Terminal: 9 a.m. Monday

From buses beached like an invasion fleet
They fill the waiting room with striding feet.

Their faces, white, and void of hate or pity,
Move on tall bodies toward the conquered city.

Among the lesser breeds of black and brown 5
They board their taxis with an absent frown,

Each to his concrete citadel,
To rule the city and to buy and sell.

At five o'clock they ride the buses back,
Leaving their Irish to guard the brown and black. 10

At six a drink, at seven dinner's served.
At ten or twelve, depressed, undressed, unnerved,

They mount their wives, dismount, they doze and dream
Apocalyptic Negroes in a stream

Of moving torches, marching from the slums, 15
Beating a band of garbage pails for drums,

Marching, with school-age children in their arms,
Advancing on the suburbs and the farms,

To integrate the schools and burn the houses . . .
The normal morning comes, the clock arouses 20

Junior and senior executive alike.
Back on the bus, and down the usual pike.

From buses beached like an invasion fleet
They fill the waiting room with striding feet.

Lew Welch

Chicago Poem

I lived here nearly 5 years before I could
    meet the middle western day with anything approaching
Dignity. It's a place that lets you
    understand why the Bible is the way it is:
Proud people cannot live here. 5

The land's too flat. Ugly sullen and big it
    pounds men down past humbleness. They
Stoop at 35 possibly cringing from the heavy and
    terrible sky. In country like this there
Can be no God but Jahweh. 10

In the mills and refineries of its south side Chicago
    passes its natural gas in flames
Bouncing like bunsens from stacks a hundred feet high.
    The stench stabs at your eyeballs.
The whole sky green and yellow backdrop for the skeleton 15
    steel of a bombed-out town.

Remember the movies in grammar school? The goggled men
    doing strong things in
Showers of steel-spark? The dark screen cracking light
    and the furnace door opening with a 20
Blast of orange like a sunset? Or an orange?

It was photographed by a fairy, thrilled as a girl, or
    a Nazi who wished there were people
Behind that door (hence the remote beauty), but Sievers,
    whose old man spent most of his life in there, 25
Remembers a "nigger in a red T-shirt pissing into the
    black sand."

It was 5 years until I could afford to recognize the ferocity.
    Friends helped me. Then I put some
Love into my house. Finally I found some quiet lakes 30
    and a farm where they let me shoot pheasant.

Standing in the boat one night I watched the lake go absolutely
    flat. Smaller than raindrops, and only
Here and there, the feeding rings of fish were visible 100 yards
    away—and the Blue Gill caught that afternoon 35
Lifted from its northern lake like a tropical! Jewel at its ear.
    Belly gold so bright you'd swear he had a
Light in there. His color faded with his life. A small
    green fish . . .

All things considered, it's a gentle and an undemanding 40
    planet, even here. Far gentler
Here than any of a dozen other places. The trouble is
    always and only with what we build on top of it.

There's nobody else to blame. You can't fix it and you
    can't make it go away. It does no good appealing 45
To some ill-invented Thunderer
    brooding above some unimaginable crag . . .

It's ours. Right down to the last small hinge it
    all depends for its existence
Only and utterly upon our sufferance. 50

Driving back I saw Chicago rising in its gases and I
    knew again that never will the
Man be made to stand against this pitiless, unparalleled
    monstrocity. It
Snuffles on the beach of its Great Lake like a 55
    blind, red, rhinocerous.
It's already running us down.

You can't fix it. You can't make it go away.
    I don't know what you're going to do about it,
But I know what I'm going to do about it. I'm just 60
    going to walk away from it. Maybe
A small part of it will die if I'm not around

    feeding it anymore.

Lew Welch

Hiking Poem / High Sierra

Measurements can never tell it:

4,000 feet down into a canyon and
4,500 feet up the other side,
in a little under 8 miles, with a
30 pound pack on my back . . . or

Several times up and down the stairs of the
Empire State Building, in
one afternoon, with
30 pound pack on my back

William Witherup

Freeway

An infected vein
carrying filth to and from the city;

a funnel
draining a huge operating table.

Even the light here 5
is the color of pus.

All the late models
have tinted windows to shield the murderers

and the chrome is honed
to slash and carve. 10

The city has complied
by drawing a rubber curtain of shrubbery

to enclose the view
and muffle the screams.

John Woods

Home Town

The home town is gone.
Tract houses correct the field
where we flew model planes in oat stubble.
A dry dream by Mondrian
squares the waving oak floor 5
of the old school,
and flattens out over the playground
where we fought for bull's rights
over home plate and silly girls.

The home town grays into old snapshots, 10
the arthritic swing sinks into the chained elm,
and the elm sinks into bad paper
announcing the imminent explosion
of a discount house.

No one comes to class with walnut-stained hands, 15
the A & P does not sell sassafras,
nor do they give away cowboy suits
at the Saturday western.

Totally insured against nostalgia,
I sentimentalize early television, 20
And munch with the children
dry leaves of cereal.

Last night, I saw de Gaulle
in his home town
defy General Motors via Telstar. 25

James Wright

From a Bus Window in Central Ohio, Just before a Thunder Shower

Cribs loaded with roughage huddle together
Before the north clouds.
The wind tiptoes between poplars.
The silver maple leaves squint
Toward the ground.
An old farmer, his scarlet face
Apologetic with whiskey, swings back a barn door
And calls a hundred black-and-white Holsteins
From the clover field.

James Wright

Today I Was So Happy, So I Made This Poem

As the plump squirrel scampers
Across the roof of the corncrib,
The moon suddenly stands up in the darkness,
And I see that it is impossible to die.
Each moment of time is a mountain.
An eagle rejoices in the oak trees of heaven,
Crying
This is what I wanted.

Curtis Zahn

Antiwarwoman

She made the skies with eyes like
Two or three wounded doves
And in a delicate mourn for peace
        Forgave them their wars
While the Generals, late for their Martinis & Olives   5
And, I suppose, destiny
Clicked shut their minds, their brief
    Cases, and called
    For Cadillacs;
Their famed, buttonpushing fingers   10
Concealed at all times
From the wistful soil of public gaze
By immaculate gloves.
        And she counted the stars
Lately to be subdivided by Nucleotheorists   15
With their perplexed mathematics of some
        Simply smashing plan
For the abolition of hunger, poverty, and world itself
While nibbling an O'Henry bar
Meant for some oriental child.   20
And now also unsure of her warmth & clothing
In that muscular affluence of cost-plus unity
She put her placard aside
And went into the restroom where unsegregated women
Sat alongside   25
The bewildered constituents of Democracy.